Know Better, Do Better

20 Steps to Empowerment and Love

Philip Allan Turner

ISBN-13: 978-0692335192

ISBN-10: 0692335196

I wish to dedicate this book to my parents whose guidance through it all has helped me to become a better man; a man closer to who God intended me to be. I thank all the people out there who have helped me along the way, and are serving the Lord and doing God's work each day. My hope is that this book glorifies God!

Understanding the internal environment and conditioning

Birth

Adulthood

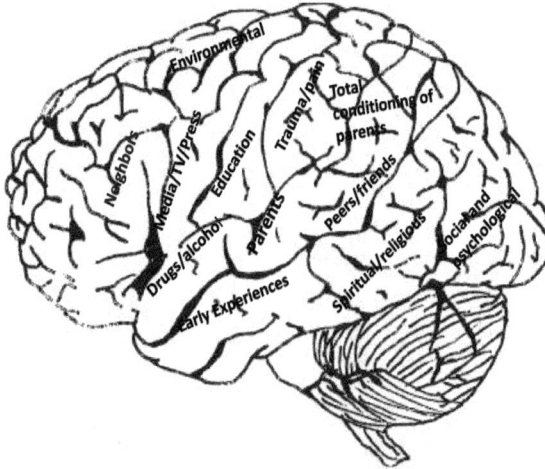

Your internal operating directive

Consist of a totality of your Beliefs, Attitudes, Behaviors, Habits from birth to adulthood

Transformation occurs by looking inward

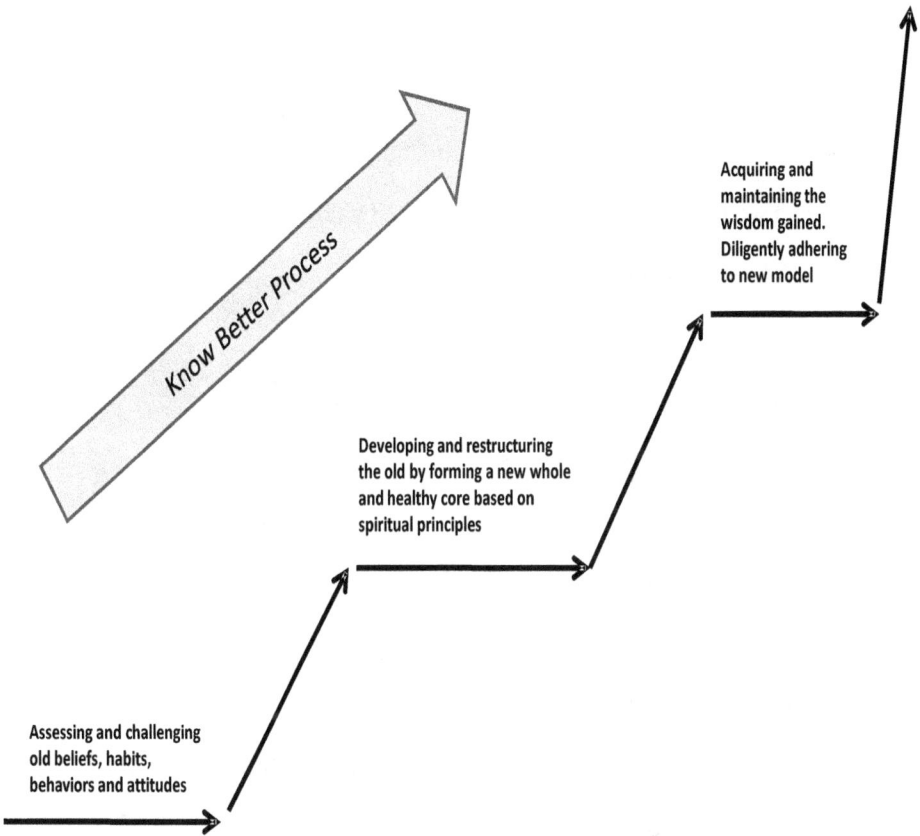

GOD

Know Better Process

Acquiring and
maintaining the
wisdom gained.
Diligently adhering
to new model

Developing and restructuring
the old by forming a new whole
and healthy core based on
spiritual principles

Assessing and challenging
old beliefs, habits,
behaviors and attitudes

KNOW BETTER, DO BETTER

"I did then what I knew how to do. Now that I know better, I do better." Maya Angelou

INTRODUCTION

I love the above Maya Angelou quote because it provides a powerful life lesson on how to live. This quote freed me and allowed me to move forward after the most difficult time in my life. I believe this quote can provide inspiration to anyone who has made a mistake or fallen down. Maya Angelou put the same thought another way when she said, "Do the best you can until you know better. Then when you know better, do better." My first book in this series is called "Know Better, Do Better – How To Lean Into The Light and Be Your Best SELF!" was written to help people have an abundant life. I got a lot of positive responses and was asked to provide a shorter version focused on the 20 steps. This book is focused on those steps. By knowing better, we can master ourselves so we can be our best self. It's easy to get off track in life and I believe this book can provide some tangible steps to get and stay on track to experience the life you were meant to live. When we know better, we can do better. When we get better, it will get better.

For many years, like some people, I lived a good life but I wasn't realizing my full potential. I was sleepwalking through life enjoying what I thought was a full life until I lost my job, went through a bad break-up after a long-term relationship. Shortly after that, the bank foreclosed on my house and a major depression came over me. In sum, my life fell apart and I felt I had nothing to live for! I wanted to end my life. It was in this pit of despair, I found that I had no real foundation or core in my life. I realized I had been a slave to my own desires. A philosopher once wrote, "Man is done or undone by his desires."

When I became depressed, I started drinking alcohol excessively and using drugs because I lost hope. Hopelessness became my norm and I was without purpose. My identity was tied to my career and through the collection of material objects so when things fell apart, I thought I lost everything. It was only when I fell to my knees that I was forced to look up. I found a way to ignite that fire within my soul and want others to understand that no matter what has happened to you, it's never too late to be who God created you to be. My story is really no different than many of yours, a universal human journey. I recognize there are other people with different mentors and paths but the path that saved my life was through the Bible and Jesus Christ.

I started reading the Bible and hundreds of self-help and psychology books. I asked myself the same questions many of you have probably asked yourselves at some point. Is this it? Why am I here? What is my purpose in life? Does my life have meaning? Will it get better? Can I gain inner happiness and joy? I wanted to know how to get out of the mental pit I found myself in so I started researching what others did to move forward. It took me three years to write this book.

While writing this work, I found happiness in the process of learning a better way. As I studied the way others found hope, I started understanding how much inner power I actually had.

From the darkness, I started pulling myself out and learned how to lean into the light to be my best self. I learned how to master myself. 'Know Better, Do Better' is a strategy in how to master ourselves. The more information we have, the better we can be. Many people allow their circumstances to negatively affect their thoughts, feelings and actions. I learned how to master my thoughts, feelings and actions; and I want to show others how to master themselves.

My story is not about what I lost but what I found, a God-consciousness. I learned God has a plan and purpose for all of us, and now my identity is through God. When I learned to effectively follow spiritual principles in my daily life, abundance started to overflow in my life. I made Jesus my life coach. I live each day with the intention of hope, faith and love now. My goal was to grow closer to God, to make God my default setting.

I want to provide a powerful verse of scripture to start you off on your new path for purpose and meaning.

> "For I know the thoughts that I think toward you, says the Lord, thoughts of peace and not of evil, to give you a future and hope. Then you will call upon Me and go and pray to Me, and I will listen to you. And you will seek Me and find Me, when you search for Me with all your heart. I will be found by you, says the Lord, and I will bring you back from your captivity (Jeremiah 29:11-14)."

This work is steeped in the teachings of the Bible; but I also use examples and parables from other spiritual traditions such as Buddhism, Hinduism, Judaism and Islam. Those believing in spirituality or a higher power can also follow the steps in this book because the underlying concepts are universal.

My story is about getting back on track and moving into the light. The Buddha said that we should, "Be your own light," and his last words were, "Strive on untiringly." In Luke 17:21, Jesus says, "...For indeed, the kingdom of God is within you." Further, Jesus says,"...I have come that they may have life, and that they may have it more abundantly (John 10:10)." We were born to have an abundant life but many, like me, get lost along the way. I provide background on how we areconditioned from birth, but through self-awareness we can become empowered and purposeful in order to live an abundant life. The diagram at the start of this work details the programming or conditioning and the framework described later in this work.

This book can be used by anyone of any faith group because I use examples from different spiritual paths.

There is so much untapped potential inside of each of us. What should you expect when you read this book? My goal is to help the reader ignite the passion inside to reach their full potential. There is hope for everyone, and there is a better way if you are living in the darkness.

The 20 steps to empowerment and love can lead to more inner balance. Each step is detailed in separate chapters using a God conscious lens. The following is what I see as a plan for living an abundant life: Spot the issues in your life; assess or analyze those issues; develop a plan and work it diligently; in order to acquire inner joy and ignite a fire inside of you. This assessment process continues throughout our lives, we need to continually assess ourselves in order to maintain balance, making adjustments along the way. I created 20 steps to allow me to live a whole and healthy life. I work my 20 steps constantly to be the man that God intends me to be. The goal is to master our mind by understanding, observing and then modifying our thinking, to align it along spiritual principles. One finds there is no path to love, love is the path. Too many people struggle with purpose and meaning in their lives.

Happiness is a choice and we all have the power inside of us to choose that internal location despite the external conditions. There are three verses of scripture that play heavily in this work and in my current life: 1) "As a man thinketh in his heart, so as he is. (Proverbs 23:7)"; 2) Jesus said, "Everything is possible for the person who believes. (Mark 9:23)"; and 3) "And you shall know the truth, and the truth shall set you free. (John 8:32)." I praise God for all that has come into my life, for without which I would not have come under this God-consciousness. I hope that this project honors God.

"The biggest human temptation is to settle for too little." Thomas Merton

To summarize, I believe that finding inner personal freedom is about breaking out of the reoccurring destructive patterns of the past. Thoughts are energy and positive thoughts produce positive energy, and the opposite is true. There are several truths I posit:

1. We are broken because of the conditioning we have gone through and the experiences we have lived.

2. There is another path, a more enlightened path.

3. Through effort and daily practice, we can break out of the programming of the past to rewire our minds to live a better life.

4. As salvation is not constant, neither is enlightenment. We must constantly strive to stay in the present moment and on the right Godly path.

God has always been there for us and is waiting for us to return to a life which demonstrates that we love Him with our whole heart. We must live our Godly nature by being conscious of our thoughts, words, and deeds. There are different doorways or paths we can choose, and too many of us actually choose pain and suffering. We must know our minds so that we are no longer led by those destructive feelings, thoughts, and actions of the past. The Buddhist believe that being mindful leads to happiness.

My premise is as easy as ABC. Abundance (will come into our lives) = Belief (deep faith in God) + Control (learning how to master ourselves).

Abundance is based on living up to our God given potential. Belief is about having steadfast faith in God. Control is focused on mastery of self through my 20 easy steps.

You are either: in control, out of control, or under control. I call my plan "20 steps to an abundant life or to empowerment and love" because it helped me to be in control of my own destiny. Once I took my spiritual, physical and mental health seriously each day, I was able to move forward to maximize my potential. The process involved throughout my journey allowed me to build a stronger spiritual core which led to inner balance using a new whole and healthy perspective so I could deal with life on life's terms.

I have attempted to create a guide with the goal of being a better, more loving and compassionate person. Too many people are waiting for God to help them, to answer their prayers but many times God has given us all we need to help ourselves. You and I are fully equipped, like a fine automobile. Further, I came to understand that "no one was coming to save me, so I would have to save myself by actively participating in my own rescue." Many people are looking for a huge miracle but the greatest miracle is overlooked by most -- each new day is a gift from God and we have an opportunity to be better than the previous day! We can start anew, striving for a higher once we understand that there is great power within us. This book will challenge you because I ask 20 'Know Better' Life Questions throughout this work.

'Know Better' Life Question: What great work were you put on the earth to create? What is your great purpose in life?

'Know Better' Life Principle: *"Don't give up; look up (at God). Live up (to your potential and destiny). Don't give in, look in (ward to see the God within you)."*

Lastly, there are 'Know Better' Empowerment Exercises to help you to do better each day.

"Man is the only animal who has to be encouraged to live." Thus Spake Zarathustra by Friedrich Nietzsche

I now see life through a God consciousness. I had always heard that the Bible was the roadmap to life, but I never viewed it that way. I was living a life which was displeasing to God according to His word. Thus, I decided to change my life by removing the bad and replacing it with a new way. There are still times that I fall short, but the difference is that I now live with a God consciousness that I did not have before.

This God consciousness has been integrated throughout all parts of my life and the relationships therein. My story is a journey of growth and transformation, your story can be the same. Make your life story, a love story.

Life can be a challenge and depending on how one views it through their internal filters is an important factor in being able to overcome these challenges. Philippians 4:13 says, "I can do all things through Christ who strengthens me." I can do all things if I believe and not worry; just give it to the God of my understanding. Through Jesus Christ, we can all be more than we were. But to be more and have an abundant life, we must follow God's commands first. Today, my worth is defined by my relationship in Christ Jesus and the love that my God has for me. My 20 steps of empowerment and love helped me to find inner balance and joy. I only have love, light and positive energy for everyone who have crossed my path. I pray that the reader finds what they are looking for in their journey.

We all have the power to change at any moment. Tomorrow is a new day where you can refuse to be encumbered with the baggage of the past.

My faith is deep and I found a better more meaningful life by following the 20 steps. I also came up with a few truths which come out of my steps and helped me to maintain both peace and inner joy.

1) God loves me unconditionally and needs me to unconditionally surrender.

2) God wants me to have a whole, healthy and abundant life.

3) This life will require me to go through some adversity, pain and disappointments.

4) From adversity, I will learn some valuable lessons.

5) It's through these lessons that I learn the real meaning of my purpose.

6) God gave me a guide book (the Bible) which will provide me with encouragement and wisdom.

7) In the Bible, God advises me to love, forgive and hope without limit.

8) If I follow the wisdom in the Bible, then my path will be easier.

9) Believe that God is guiding me to a greater end.

10) Search diligently for the lesson in every moment God is trying to show me with an open, obedient and willing heart.

11) Have faith that God is in charge and that He has a plan for our lives.

12) Stay in constant daily; and even hourly communication with God through prayer and meditation, and doors will come open.

James Allen stated in *As a Man Thinketh, "Dream lofty dreams, and as you dream, so shall you become."*

Tell yourself, "**Today I will be better than yesterday. Today I will strive to move forward."**

I use many uplifting and inspiring quotes throughout this book to reinforce certain themes. With God, we can all have strength for today and bright hope for tomorrow. Hang on because your new journey is about to start!

Chapter 1

20 steps to Empowerment and Love

My aim was to create a 'Know Better' empowerment life-plan composed of easy 20 steps for living a joy filled life of abundance with love at its core. This work is inspired for my love of God, to show people how to activate the love inside. Some say that our natural state is love, and we must have to return to that place. I realized that I did not know how to love myself or anyone else in a whole and healthy manner before I started this process of growth. I had to train myself to love myself completely as well as others. Loving one's self in a healthy manner requires an enormous amount of development and intentionality. The world as we know it will not help us so we have to help ourselves. The reality TV shows and tabloid media only make it more difficult to know what true love is. Dysfunctional love sells in the media and in the tabloids today. The more dysfunctional a relationship is on TV, the better for ratings. Those crazy TV shows are conditioning and programming us to make crazy, normal. I'm tired of living in a personal 'crazy-ville'. I want to be a better man who serves God in spirit and in truth. If we do not love ourselves, how can we love others? Loving others become difficult, if there is no love in us. One can't love a little.

'Know Better' Life Principle: **If we get better, it will get better.**

'Know Better' Life Principle: **There is no path to love, love is the path.**

Being human is complicated because we make life difficult. By retraining ourselves, we can have find peace through love. The way to a deep, inner peace is through love. The below steps may help you find that inner peace and balance I have found.

> 1 - Be good to yourself. Be gentle to yourself. Love yourself by challenging yourself.

> 2 - Change your inner and outer dialogue. Change how you speak to others and how you speak to yourself. Speak with only love and kindness. Do not use self-limiting words such as "can't" or "try" either do or don't do.

> 3 - Don't limit God or God's most precious creation: You. You have unlimited power to do anything. Have and live a larger, God-inspired dream each day. Believe!

> 4 - Work out daily in three areas: physical, mentally and spiritually. (Physical exercise, meditation and prayer)

> 5 - Be positive always. Say only positive words to others and especially yourself. Eliminate all negativity and negative people in your lives.

6 - Have specific, measurable plans/goals and dreams. Write it down and chart your growth in three areas: spiritual, mental and physical.

7 - Smile, it helps bring you joy. Keep joy in your heart despite your external circumstances.

8 - Help others, volunteer. Sow seeds of love. Be a blessing to others daily. Be a light for others.

9 - Understand who you are, what you are and how much power you have inside through how God sees you. God is within us and has given us the power to be whatever we want to be.

10 - Love God!!! Love everyone especially yourself. Let your love show through your actions. Do everything with love. Loving others is not judging them.

11 - Forgive everyone especially yourself. Eject any ill will or negative bias you have against anyone in your life.

12 - Show compassion and kindness to everyone especially yourself.

13 - Do not judge anyone especially yourself. Leave judgment to God. With all of our faults and mistakes, we are in no position to judge anyone.

14 - Believe that you can change and then work towards that change ambitiously. Believe that it has already happened.

15 - Read the Bible, devotional and/or another great religious book daily.

16 - Attend a house of worship weekly.

17 - Have faith! Faith and fear both require that we believe in something that we can't see. Fear and faith are opposing muscle groups and can't be flexed at the same time.

18 - Think good and pure thoughts. Always have honest intentions. You can change your life by changing your thinking.

19 - Do everything with passion. Live with an inner fire. Live your passions daily.

20 - Pray Big, Love Big and Hope Big; and do all three Boldly!

In looking for ways to serve and honor God, I decided to see where I deviated and how I could return to a path which was pleasing to God. Before I returned to God, I had to analyze the areas where I needed work. For example, I had to change the way I viewed love. It's easy to love those who love me, but to love others as Jesus commands can be a challenge. To love those who are completely different from us or those who are mean or misguided is a challenge because of our past conditioning. I came to understand that I had a love problem. We believe love requires knowledge. We usually love people once we learn about them but if we are truly obedient then we would love others as God commands us unconditionally.

We can condemn the sin but we should love the sinner. I came to realize how unlike Jesus Christ I was in my everyday life, and this awareness allowed me to move closer to God.

'Know Better' Life Question: In your everyday life, are you moving closer to God?

I had to ask myself, am I striving each day to be better by being intention to move closer to God? Am I striving to be holy and righteous in my daily walk for God? I looked inside and found myself lacking so I composed a list of areas which I found hard/challenging and simple/easy:

-Being thankful always is a challenge, while complaining is easy.

-Loving others as we love ourselves is a challenge, while judging others is easy.

-Forgiving others is a challenge, while holding grudges is easy.

-Showing compassion and kindness to others is a challenge, while being indifferent to others is easy.

-Staying in communication with God through constant prayer is a challenge, while looking at worldly guidance is easy.

-Trusting God is a challenge, while distrusting is easy.

-Being patient and expressing loving-kindness always is a challenge, while getting upset is easy.

By looking at the above problem areas in my life, I was able to start the process of restructuring my inner person. So for me now, I am more self-aware and that which was challenging is now easier. Those things which I did easily in the past, I now challenge myself to be better. I now choose to be live differently. I came to this conclusion after I identified those issues in my life which I needed to improve. I examined myself, which was painful at times but I matured because of the process. Examine yourself with an open heart to become the person God wants you to become.

Once I changed my prayers, then my world view changed. I started asking God to use me and to show me where I can be used. I started asking God to give everyone joy/peace on the inside. I prayed that everyone have inner joy especially those who I thought of as my enemies. I now pray that everyone becomes closer to God as I have. Like the story in the Bible where the man who was lowered in the house through the roof and was healed by Jesus, I had to do something radical to be healed--have unwavering faith. Too many have faith during the church service but after they return to their broken and defeated life of sadness and joylessness. I realized that hope was necessary to live, and I believe God's word when He said that I should choose life.

The Power: In the list of 7 areas above, I originally had used the word "difficult" instead of challenging but realized that its only as difficult as I made it or as easy as I made it. It's my choice to accept things are being difficult or easy; challenging or simple. I realized that I had the power. I decided to use the power by believing each day would be positive and enriching experience; and thus, that is what I had. Some choose to believe that each day is a curse from God or a plague to be endured, living a defeated life each day. Some see every little problem as an insurmountable mountain while others see the potential lesson which will make them better. We all need to look for the lesson from God which will make their lives better.

The Path: I decided to look at my spiritual walk and focus on the areas which would be love-centered path allowing me to grow. There is a path, and I was on the wrong path because it was an external path. I used to look to external things to make me happy and feel a measure of joy. I am now on a path, a path from within based on love, God centered and focused.

Henry Blackaby said, "*If you have an obedience problem (obedience to God), you have a love problem.*"

If we focus on loving God with all our heart, soul, mind and strength then we will want to obey God. God is love, so how can we believe we are following God when we do not love. I love how the Psalmist put it in 32:10, "Unfailing love surrounds whose trust in the Lord."

John Algeo explained, *"the path exists within us."*

Spanish Poet Antonio Machado stated, *"Traveler, there is no trail; you make the trail by walking it."*

I think that both of the above quotes with seemingly differing views are true. God is within us as Apostle John says in 1 John 4:4; and we make our own path by pressing forward as Paul states in Philippians 3:12-14. The paths are found by seeking wisdom through a divine source but the world provides no path to those who are seeking. Reality shows (not all but the negative, ego-filled ones), tabloid media who focuses on the negative aspects of society and other negative paths take us away from God. The world challenges us because it puts value on the ungodly, not the Godly. The Godly is ridiculed and perversion is promoted and exploited such as in the Jerry Springer show or those shows watch it.

The guidebook: My mother told me the Bible is our roadmap to life. She was so right and explained to me that every problem known to man is in the Bible. I didn't listen when I was younger but once I was brought to my knees and forced to look up, I found beauty through Jesus Christ. I found love, beauty and purpose in the 66 divinely inspired books of the Bible. I found meaning and learned how I could thrive in any situation. I found hope, love and beauty. The

Bible says that hope never disappoints. Hope is God. God is love and love is found in those who love God. Jesus tells us that love is the fulfillment of the law. Loving others is not what many music videos promote. The anger filled music from some artist today say people should love money, women and material things. There is no meaning found in loving things; we must love God, ourselves and others. There is a unique shaped void inside of us which can only be filled by Godly love, a love of God and of others.

Love: I realized that I had to throw out much of what I had known previously about love in order to live a spiritual life, a life pleasing to God. I had to learn how to love and how to be loved in a healthy and whole manner. I needed to learn to love God and others using a better template, a template centered on how God viewed love. I had to retrain myself to learn how to be loved as well. I was used to being loved in a defective manner but now I realize what it healthy and what is not healthy. The Bible tells us that love is the fulfillment of the law. John the Apostle said, "How can you say you love God whom you do not see, when you do not love your neighbor whom you do see." He goes on further to say, "You are a liar if you say you love God and do not love your neighbor (1 John 4:20)." Love covers a multitude of sins to include forgiveness. Mother Teresa has said, "*The grace of God is not in you as long as you do not forgive.*" Love helps to guide us if we are open to the love of God in our lives. Most people do not know how to love or to be loved. The Bible can help us to learn about healthy love especially in chapters like 1 Corinthians 13 written by the Apostle Paul.

God has given us a compass on how to traverse the hills and valleys in life. Both the hills and the valleys are so important to help us mature into spiritual people. Mother Teresa explains that we will suffer and if we are going to suffer, then let us suffer cheerfully. Reading the Bible helps us to live a life of meaning without guessing at life. I think my story is about what I found through reading the Bible and listening to wisdom from other great teachers like the Buddha. God is love and love can heal. My story is about who I was and who I came to be. After I started to write down what I learned, I begin to feel more whole. So many of the tales of old discuss the hero's journey, after great struggles and failings, find love. I found love in and through, God.

Joy Mills of the Theosophical Society (TS) explained it so elegantly, "*knowing who and what we are, and with our destiny in our own hands, we are at peace within and have the courage to face the challenges before us.*" I found that deeply profound and accurate vis-a-vis my journey. In the *Masters, the Voice of the Silence*, it stated, "*Prepare thyself, for thou wilt have to travel on alone. The teacher can but prepare the way. The path is one for all, the means to reach the goal must vary with the pilgrims.*" There are many paths.

I believe that many hear the truth but decide to ignore the truth. Ignoring the truth will only bring sorrow. Jesus said that you shall know the truth and the truth shall set you free. Freedom brings joy and contentment. I found that there were many traditions which provided guidance. Tim Boyd, the national president of the TS provided some valuable insight, "*The challenge before us will also be the same - to see the world with fresh eyes and to treat each moment as precious and extraordinary. May we rise to meet this challenge."* The challenge is before us, it's our choice and love is the path.

"You were put on this earth to achieve your greatest self, to live out your purpose, and to do it courageously."   Dr.   Steve   Maraboli

Chapter 2

Step One: *Being good and gentle with yourself starts with a process of recovery.*

This first step is about becoming intentional in how we live each day. Too many of us beat ourselves up each day over the mistakes of the past. We relive that trauma over and over, in effect becoming our own worst enemy. Be good to yourself, leave the past in the past. It matters not what others think about you but how what you think about yourself.

Louise Hay stated, *"I find that when we really love and accept and approve of ourselves exactly as we are, then everything in life works."* This quote describes what step one is trying to convey. To further explain this concept I want to use a quote from Eleanor Roosevelt, *"No one can make you feel inferior without your consent."* This whole book is about empowerment and attempting to show you how you have the power to be more than you are. This first step is vital in moving forward to the life of abundance that God wants for you.

My recovery is the most important thing in my life, recovery from being programmed to love the things of this world instead of things of God. Your recovery must be your number one goal each day. My goal is to be whole and healthy, and having whole and healthy relationships in my life. I look at my awakening and subsequent recovery as finally being good to myself. In being good to myself, I determined that I needed to focus on loving others and being compassionate to others. I have more compassion now than ever because I now view helping others as a way to help myself. I make my personal recovery my number one goal in my life. I call it tending to my own garden because if I am not whole and healthy then I can't be good to anyone else.

It starts with becoming more self-aware and conscious of your thoughts, words and actions each day. I used to be selfish when it came to my needs, my wants and my desires but now I am focused on being good to myself in a whole and healthy manner while looking at the world through a God-Consciousness lens. There are times when one must be selfish to move forward. For example, sometimes we have to leave those frienemies (friend-enemies) and all the other toxic people behind. We may have to love them from afar and pray for them with love in our hearts for them. Some relationships are not good for us and we need to realize this when we start to become self-aware.

I realize that when a person lives in the darkness, it's hard to see the light. Many people live in partial darkness and partial light but over time the darkness encroaches on the area of light. Even living in partial darkness prevents us from getting closer to God, and being the people who God wants us to be. The Bible discusses in James 1:8 that, "A double minded man is unstable in all his ways." Too many of us are not committed to being our best self. We must believe what God says about us, God only makes masterpieces and we are one of His creations! If we start from a place of obedience and willingness while aligning ourselves to something greater than our own ego, we can be more. Our pride and ego has gotten us off the mark. We need to look at doing things differently because we want a different result.

If you don't know the internal environment that you are living in, then you have already lost. I believe that Buddhist philosophy encapsulates the internal environment we find ourselves in these days. The Buddhist believes in four noble truths. I am not going to go into all of them now but just touch on the first one in this section.

The first noble truth say that to live is to suffer: aging and illness is suffering, not to get what you want is suffering, living with something that you do not desire is suffering, wanting is a part of suffering. The Buddha believed that we live in a world where our desires cause us to suffer. k.d. Lang has a song called "constant craving" and it talks about how constant craving has always been. We all want more. We suffer because we want more. We crave for things to be different than they are. Pain in life is a given and when we resist this basic fact then we suffer more. The Bible discusses how we should not be attached to worldly things but first seek the Kingdom of God (Mathew 6:33). We are told by Jesus in 6th chapter of Mathew that we should not be anxious about our life. So many people live an anxiety filled life every minute of the day. Jesus tells us in the same 6th chapter of Mathew, "You cannot serve God and money." This first noble truth is mirrored and expanded on in the New Testament. John wrote, "Do not love the world or the things in the world. If anyone loves the world, the love of the Father is not in him. For all that is in the world -- the desires of the flesh and the desires of the eyes and pride in possessions -- is not from the Father but is from the world. And the world is passing away along with its desires, but whoever does the will of God abides forever (1 John 2:15-17)."

The Bible opens our eyes to the truth and gives us guidance of what to do when we find out the world is not what we have been told. We are all told many stories while growing up. We learn information from our parents, friends and teachers throughout our developmental phases. This is part of the conditioning process which I have addressed separately. But in sum, we are conditioned through life but I posit that we have been defectively conditioned and trained.

We find out that there is no Santa at a young age and later we find out that the world is not always nice, just or fair. We arrive in this world thinking that good guys wear white hats and bad guys wear black hats while curling their handlebar mustache. We believe that good will always triumph over evil, and that people will eventually do the right thing. But through living in the world, we are then re-educated. We realized that what we were told was not exactly correct. Sometimes it appears that the bad guys win and injustice prevails in the world but I believe in a just God who will reward all those who are steadfast. I believe that there are things in this universe that we can never know but I have faith in God.

We constantly fight with the notions we have in our heads. We are not all created equal because we all have different gifts but we can all equally use our gifts to glorify God. We find out that some are more equal or others have better or more gifts than we have. We realize that the world is unfair and that sometimes others get away with evil while the good encounters troubles. We come to understand that life does not always give us roses. This is when the first test comes. We can become embittered and let it affect our lives in a negative manner or we can use those failings, defeats and tragedies to make us better people. Don't be bitter, be better!

Within our perceived defects of character and weaknesses lies the key to realizing our true strength. By facing our shortcomings, the fears and the problems which come into our lives routinely, we can discover a feeling of joy and peace which extends outward.

Most people get use to this endless cycle of discontent. Too few people are happy or even know how to find joy outside of collecting material objects. Happiness comes from opening one's heart, not closing it. We must strive to move forward each day.

Helen Keller once wrote, *"You will succeed if you persevere; and you will find a joy in overcoming obstacles."*

I never realized some very important truths until later in my life, specifically when I found myself on my knees after many disappoints came into my life within one year. I never realized how important love is until after I read the New Testament and learned how much God loved each of us. I never knew my true worth because I measured my worth based on the world I lived in, which was not 'of God' but I have learned now how to view my self-worth through the eyes of God. Love is the key to a glorious life. Love is a fire which should burn inside for our God and for each other. I now find peace in what I have especially when I ask God to show me the way each morning. I find peace when I ask God to teach me the lesson in every moment. I find contentment when I ask God to use me for His purpose, not mine.

The Bible says that, "God has not given us the spirit of fear but... of love and of a sound mind." We just need to return to our sound mind by loving. We can recover by awakening to basic truths to our current reality. At the moment of the Buddha's awakening under the Bodhi tree, he declared, "How strange, all beings possess the capacity to be awakened, to understand, to love, to be free, yet allow themselves to be carried away on the ocean of suffering."

Life is a journey and is full of adventures. I found that once I started communicating with God throughout the day asking God what He was trying to show me in a particular moment then life became easier. I no longer allowed my ego to lead me in various situations but God's desires to lead me instead. I allowed love to be in my heart regardless of the exterior circumstances. My new God-consciousness allowed me to view things differently, with compassion and loving-kindness. This was hard to do at first as my human conditioned mind wanted to judge me and everyone else. That inner judge often tormented me at every opportunity. I think that we all know that the inner judge can be as cruel as we allow it. The inner critic is the voice of shame, blame, resentment, anger, belittlement, fear, contempt and hatred. But once we understand that the little voice does not control us but that we control that little voice, then life becomes manageable and full of hope. I had to silence that inner critic of myself and for everyone else. I use new God-consciousness lens to view my actions and the actions of others. My God-conscious lenses only views life through love.

I did not appreciate the painful process of my journey at first but learned that the process was important and could not be rushed. In growing vegetables in a garden, the process can't be rushed. The same with raising a child, one can't feed a newborn whole steak. The journey and process offers knowledge and insight that can transform our dreams and aspirations into reality. If we walk the path looking for direction from God, then the path becomes the great teacher. Our path must be one of love. The path may have a lot of dips and curves and unexpected turns but they help to guide us to a better path, a more abundant path. We can use these paths as opportunities to work with our mind. All the mistakes and difficulties are vital to our awakening.

In Sun Tzu's *The Art of War*, one of the principles in the book makes it clear that we start the process of forming and transforming by creating victorious conditions first in ourselves. It asks us to recognize how we conduct ourselves and interact with others communicates an enormous amount to the world around us. Just by walking around, we change the world. Being good oneself is the first step.

I am first and foremost a devote Christian, a disciple of Christ. But I see that there is great wisdom which can found from other traditions. According to the Historical Buddha, true happiness can only be found within. The Bible tells us that God is within us in 1 John 4:6. So, I can see the parallel nature of that Christian belief with the Buddhist's philosophy and discover that happiness is found through the God within each of us. The Buddhist believe that once we connect with our basic heart of sanity, calm our mind and relax then life starts to become clearer. We then can contemplate what we truly desire and what our options are for accomplishing our goals. Next we translate that into action by making a plan and executing it step by step with an attitude of kindness towards ourselves and others. In this way, we can bring a clear sense of insight and equanimity into any stressful situation.

Buddhist teacher Sakyong Mipham Rinpoche stated it very clearly, *"to move forward in daily life, we must be steady and brave. To create this bravery inside, we must learn how to handle our mind. Knowing this, the warrior practices meditation every day to know his mind and harness its energy for the good of all. If we are so busy that we do not even have a felling for our mind, meditation is the first step toward developing that feeling."*

The great Buddhist teacher Thich Nhat Hanh stated in an article about why so many find it hard to love themselves. He stated that, *"there is a habit within ourselves of looking for happiness elsewhere than in the here and now. We lack the capacity to realize that happiness is possible in the here and now, that we already have enough conditions to be happy right now."* I found philosophy to be amazingly healthy for me while I was incarcerated. He further explains, *"Love is to be kind to yourself, to be compassionate to yourself, to generate images of joys, and to look at everyone with eyes of equanimity and non-discrimination...."* When people love each other, the distinction, the limits, the frontier between them dissolve, and they become one with the person they love. There's no longer and jealousy or anger, because if they are angry at the other person, they are angry at themselves.

We are programmed to search for happiness in life but too many of us start from a defective place looking for the wrong thing in the hopes that it will fill that void. We don't truly wish the best for our adversaries like we should. Having honest intentions for every aspect in our lives helps us in being good to ourselves as it releases positive energy into the universe.

Ridgzin Jigme Lingpa explains it this way, *"The essence of loving-kindness is wishing joy for others. Like a loving mother for her child, serve others by offering all, your body, wealth, and merits, and bear all the hurts caused by them."* While some may read this with an unloving and judging eye, I read the above passage hoping to attain that level of loving-kindness for others.

There are painful feelings, strong emotions and other negative emotions that make us afraid. If we put more energy into being mindful then we learn to live with these difficult feeling without running away or judging. The Buddha taught that what we dwell upon becomes the shape of our mind. If we dwell on ill will, directed outwardly or inwardly in the form of blame or disparagement, it will become the shape of our mind until we see that it is flawed or defective. We need to liberate ourselves from judging others and ourselves. The judgmental mind needs kindness and understanding. We need to be good and gentle with ourselves in every aspect of ourselves.

I met a Sufi mystic once and was motivated to learn more about them. The Sufis have a tradition which says our thoughts should pass through three gates. Sufi's are Islamic mystics. At the first gate, we ask of our thought, "is it true?" If so, we let the thought pass through to the second gate and ask, "Is it necessary or useful?" If this is the case then we move to the third gate and ask, "Is this thought rooted in love and kindness?" Judgmental thoughts are neither true, helpful nor kind and should be stopped at the mental gates. Many Zen teachers have promoted that liberation begins with being compassionate with ourselves. By meditating even for a short while each day, we steady ourselves in moving towards an enlightened consciousness by connecting body and mind. This section was written to start you on the path of being intentionally good to yourself each day.

"Don't let the behavior of others destroy your inner peace." Dalai Lama

Let's move on to step two.

Chapter 3

Step Two: *Change your inner and outer dialogue. Change how you speak to others and how you speak to yourself. Speak with only love and kindness. Do not use self-limiting words such as "can't" or "try" either do or do not.*

There is a saying which states, *"Watch your thoughts, for they become words; choose your words, for they become actions; understand your actions, for they become habits; study your habits, for they become your character; and develop your character, for it becomes your destiny."* I found this saying to be most enlightening. I had come to believe that our thoughts can change the world and that piece of wisdom confirmed my belief. We need to listen to our thoughts and eliminate the negative thoughts while nurturing the positive ones. It seems so simple when I looked at it: Thoughts to words to actions to habits to character which all lead to our destiny. I realized for the first time that I had an internal voice.

My fear is now suppressed because of my faith in God. Today, my inner voice still tells me that there is no fear because of my deep and passionate foundation in Christ Jesus. In the past, my inner voice did not have a spiritual component to it. My inner voice was focused on putting negative in the world and I came to reap all that negative energy.

When I became a new creation in Christ Jesus, my nature changed. I was able to change my nature by changing that inner dialogue with myself. I decided to stop listening to the world and decided to focus on God's word. I found a better way through reading and internalizing the Bible. Like a compass, the Bible always points us in the right direction. I developed what I called my 20 steps to empowerment and love using God's Positioning System (GPS) to lead me back to God.

Changing my nature was a major part of living a different life. Changing my nature also involved speaking only with kindness and love to myself and others. I decided that showing love and kindness to me would involve retraining myself.

This step requires a great leap for many. The leap concerns love. One must love themselves in order to make a routine of speaking with love to themselves and to others. This step focuses on reinforcing positivity in one's life. We need to make sure that we provide a nurturing environment for ourselves and for others. If we put good in the world then it will also positively affect our lives.

'Know Better' Life Question: Do your words uplift and edify others? Do you words uplift yourself?

Psychologists say our self-worth is often based upon what we believe the most important people in our lives think of us. The problem with this principle is that people are just as flawed and defective as we are. Our actions are a clear indication as to who we are. How we write, walk and talk all says a lot about how we think. The battle is on the inside and too many people fight the wrong battles each day. Mastery of self is the key.

'Know Better' Life Principle: **You are not beyond repair because it's never too late to begin again. With God in your life, anything is possible.**

This is your life and you are the star in your own movie. You are the producer, director and writer of your life story. You can make it into anything you want by starting with how you speak with yourself and others. Here is something to ponder, when you talk bad or negative to others, you also hear the same negative words coming back into your life. Life is like a mirror and when you look into the mirror, it looks back at you. When you curse others, those same curses are heard by you and come back into your life.

'Know Better' Life Principle: **Life is a journey of infinite possibilities, why limit yourself before you even start the race in earnest.**

Life is meant to be a journey of growth and evolution. Once you start to speak blessings over others and yourself, the universe rushes to meet you. Being faithfully positive in all of your thoughts, words and deeds allow you to bring the same into your life.

Many people belittle themselves or others. Don't invalidate yourself by putting yourself in a prison of your own making. Anais Nun stated, "*We don't see things as they are, we see them as we are.*" If we uplift our words and start to understand how the universe works to align our thoughts and words with our destiny then we would all change. Putting self-imposed limitations on ourselves, then we get limited results. Eliminating all negative self-talk should be the first goal. The second goal is to eliminate all negative comments to others. Both of these goals will be a challenge because many people have programmed themselves with defaults. For example when something happens unexpectedly bad, some people say, "Oh, this always happens to me." There are some who say these types of comments so often that they do not even hear it anymore.

Polonius says in Shakespeare's Hamlet, "*To thy own self be true*". This should take on increased significance as one cannot be true to oneself when one puts down oneself or others. This is learned behavior. Don't allow your demons to dictate your life or those close to you. If you are rigorously positive in your thoughts and words, your life will begin to change for the better.

We hold great creative power inside of us. Anyone can access this power as long as they look inside. Having daily positive rituals make all the difference in that it set a pattern.

Our thoughts and our words can provide the positive or negative energy for success or failure in our lives. We don't know all the mysteries of the universe. Some things that happen to us, we bring on ourselves. If we train our minds to eliminate all negative thoughts, words or actions then our lives would be transformed into abundant and joyous vessels for God. We would live a life of heaven on earth. We would live without wars and a new higher level of existence would be possible. The Bible talks about a new Jerusalem at the end of days, that is possible once we break out of the prisons of our minds. There is a war going on inside each one of us. The war is against pride and ego, selfishness, hatred, prejudice, anger, envy and other negative forces.

Success or failure in life is based on how we think. Winners constantly think -- I will, I can, I am -- while those who do not win often point fingers and blame others for why life is not as the way they want it. Winners find a way to achieve their goals and are not dissuaded to not stop until they reach their goal. Their inner and outer dialogues are positive, all the time. If we think little goals then that is what will enter our life while if we think of big goals or achievements then we are more likely to reach the desired result. Our choices make our future.

William Shakespeare tells us, *"there is nothing either good or bad, thinking makes it so."* I know people who will start to blast Shakespeare for this or that while ignoring the wisdom. Too few people fight the right battle, the battle to break out of the prison of the mind. Many people are fighting the wrong battles each day, expending their energies in the wrong and unproductive directions.

Blaise Pascal reminds us that our achievements of today are but a sum total of our thoughts of yesterday. We are today where our thoughts of yesterday have brought us and will be tomorrow where the thoughts of today take us. In Isaiah 26:3, we learn that God will keep us in perfect peace whose mind is stayed on Him. God understands that if our thoughts are base or on worldly things then are actions will follow thus so. This is why so much is written in the Bible about changing our thoughts. In Romans 12:2 we learn from Paul, "Be not conformed to this world, but be ye transformed by the renewing of your mind." This is why we need the Spirit of God operating and moving in our hearts and minds. This can only happen when we change the inner and outer dialogue.

Messed up minds leads to messed up lives and broken families. God changed me because I opened my heart fully and completely. I decided to try something new and was rewarded.

When you make "can't" and "try" active parts of your vocabulary then you have already failed. This step is about actively helping yourself succeed by changing your inner and outer vocabulary. From the Star Wars movies, Yoda stated, *"Try not. Do or do not. There is no try."* When we try, we set ourselves up for defeat. Do your best and always seek to accomplish your goal. The old Nike commercial was right, "just do it." I love that phrase because it's about doing, not trying. Some people set themselves up for failure but saying, "I'm going to try." Saying that you will try leaves too much doubt in the outcome. Do, and if you don't hit the mark then it's okay but don't start a task by saying I'm going to try. Start by saying, "I'm going to do this and hit the mark." If you don't succeed then go to step one and be good to yourself by saying I did my best. Remember what the Apostle Paul said in Philippians 4:13, "I can do all things through Christ, who strengthens me." Paul didn't say that I can try all things. Leave no room for doubt.

Your inner and outer dialogue should focus on thoughts and words of abundance and love. You can and will succeed if you have the power of God in your mind and heart, and God is love. Like a computer program, we can only get out of the program what we put in it. Everyone needs to ask God to reprogram their hearts and minds. We need to take the junk out of our mind and heart and put in Galatians 5, 1 Corinthians 13, Proverbs 3 and the 27th Psalm into our mental computers.

Have you ever wondered why some people "get it" and others do not? I believe that it's because of they have changed their inner and outer dialogue. If you want God to bless your life, then you must ask God to fix your mind. This starts with doing your part.

'Know Better' Empowerment Exercise: Whenever you start an unhealthy dialogue in your mind I want you to say the following out loud. "Unhealthy thoughts – stop. I know better so now I can do better. I'm stronger than this, God made me an overcomer."

'Know Better' Empowerment Exercise: Whenever you have an uplifting, loving and encouraging thought about those around you, let them how you feel in new and radical loving ways. Communicate openly with love to your family, friends and love ones.

Chapter 4

Step Three: *Don't limit God or His most precious creation: You. You have unlimited power to do anything. Have and live a larger, God-inspired dream each day. Believe!*

Winston Churchill stated, *"You create your own universe as you go along."* The Bible tells us in the Gospels about how much power we have. Mathew 21:22 states, "Whatever you shall ask in prayer, believing, you shall receive." Mark 11:24 reads as thus, "Whatever things you desire, when you pray, believe that you have received them and you shall have them." In Mark 9:23 Jesus says, "All things are possible to the one who believes." The Buddha stated, *"All wrong doing arises because of the mind. If the mind is transformed can wrong doing remain?"* These above quotes show us the correct path.

Do you know who you are? You are God's greatest creation! 1 Corinthians 3:16 tells us about ourselves and the power inside of us. "Do you not know that you are the temple of God and that the Spirit of God dwells within you." These are powerful words and it's on us to believe these words.

The battle is either won or lost in your mind. You have the power and the choice. Many people already lost because they live a powerless life, a defeated life. Some of us see every day as problem or another issue to deal with instead of as a gift. These people often are just making it. We can choose the type of life we want but many of us choose to live below our Godly inheritance.

You have the power and you can choice. Wallace D. Wattles put it this way, *"There is the principle of power in every person. By the intelligent use and direction of this principle, man can develop his own mental faculties. Man has an inherent power by which he may grow in whatsoever direction he pleases, and there does not appear to be any LIMIT to the possibilities of his growth."*

God wants all of us to be whole and happy and live an abundant live. Each of us should understand how we each work. How can you operate a car if you do not understand how itworks. Although many of us have lived for 20, 30, 40 or 50 years, we still do not know how to maximize our own talents and skills fully. We all have different talents. Romans 12:6 states, "We all have different gifts, according to the grace given to each of us." It is important to believe the word of God so we can transform ourselves into being more Christ-like.

'Know Better' Life Question: When will you ignite that fire within? How long will it take you to control your emotions, direct your own will and transform your lives? Do you believe it's possible? If the answer to this question is yes; then take the necessary steps to be who God created you to be.

In your mind, you must believe that there are some mysteries that you will never understand. If you are going to believe in the internal light switch that you can flip on then it's time to turn it on. Believe anything is possible.

'Know Better' Life Principle: **God can and will change your life, God is restoring you, God is preparing you for something greater. Believe that God's dreams for you are great. God has equipped you with everything you will need to be great and to live a life of purpose and meaning.**

In Step two, I explained how changing the inner and outer dialogue can help you achieve your dreams. Tony Dungy, the first African American to win a Super Bowl as a head coach stated in his book *Uncommon* that *"Our words can uplift and heal and empower - or not. Words can inspire, rekindle a sense of wonder, and provide direction, or they can dampen spirits, condemn ideas, and destroy initiative."*

Step 3 builds on step 2 because our words and thoughts can limit us or free us to go on and do great and wondrous things. If someone came up to you and said that "You are not able to compose that piece of music, or you can't write that book, or you can't get that job, or you can't run that marathon, or you can't live healthier by choosing to eat healthier or working out daily, or you can't live for Christ by changing the way you think or the way you act" -- you would probably get upset if someone told you these things. Many people tell themselves these same types of negative statements every day whether consciously or subconsciously. Consciously, they say things like, "I can't lose weight or I can't run a marathon," but by saying this or thinking this, you have limited yourself already. Subconsciously, people just do not make an effort in such a way that will guarantee success. God wants us to do great things!

If we fail then it was just an experiment to get us to our ultimate destination in a better manner. Thomas Edison stated, *"I have not failed. I've just found 10,000 ways that won't work."* Edison also said, *"Many of life's failures are people who did not realize how close they were to success when they gave up."* Failure helps us to gain valuable knowledge in order to succeed later. Many people are discouraged by failure and then they just stop trying.

Limits are put on us by society but many times we continue to put them on ourselves. Steve Job's had the amazing vision when he told colleagues that it was not the consumer's job to tell them what they wanted but instead it was their job to tell the consumer what they needed. This was revolutionary because other companies convened focus groups in order to see what the consumers liked or did not like. Steve Jobs believed that it was his job to tell the consumer what they wanted.

The world is one of infinite and limitless possibilities where you can live an amazing wonderful life; or it's a world of limits and boundaries which limit you to live a mediocre and unfulfilled life. The Bible says that tomorrow is not promised to us. We need to take advantage of every opportunity that is given to us each day. Aristotle said that, *"We can't learn without pain."* This is great wisdom because all of my failures have made me a better, more compassionate person.

One of the keys to life is to not allow life's failures or disappointments limit you from becoming the person that God wants you to be. God has no limits and we are God's greatest creation, created by the very breath of God.

'Know Better' Life Principle: **Our spirits are limitless and there is no limit to how much we can love. There has not been a measurement to how much love the human heart can hold.**

God is love and the Bible says that we are to love God with all our heart, mind and soul; and to love our neighbor as our self. Love is the fulfillment of the law. If we are not loving God and loving others then we are not living as Jesus wants us to live.

I believe that "the devil is content to let us profess Christianity as long as we do not practice it." Too many people claim to be Christians while too few people actually live a life for God through their daily walk.

We are given limits at a very young age when an adult or teacher says, "you can't be a lawyer or a doctor." We then internalize that limited thinking. There were even worse examples in some people's youth when their parents said, "you'll never be anything," or "your father didn't amount to anything and neither will you," or "your mother was an addict and you'll be the same." Many statements like the above were heard by kids growing up and the conditioning process of limiting our outlook on life starts imprinting inside. Other people start to limit themselves at some point because of disappointments or heartbreak. Don't believe you are worthless or cursed because you are a child of God. Don't put your dreams in a little box or forgot about your ambitions. Some people just start to drift in life. Drifting is another way to subconscious limit yourself. Many people drift spiritually from God and begin a life of learned aimlessness. They become trained in living a hectic life without reflection.

There are many people who believe in Murphy's Law which says, "if anything can go wrong, it will." These people's vision is constrained by an acceptance of limits. They say this so often that it fails to register as being a self-imposed limit. To retrain ourselves, we need to see everything as a step in another direction which will help us to get closer to another goal. There was a story I heard about a young boy was injured in a farming accident by a faulty machine. His parents were mystics and believed that everything happened for a reason. The boy was injured but recovered but in the investigation of the machine it was learned that if the machine was not serviced and fixed then there would have been an explosion that would have killed the boy and his brothers along with the father. That accident prevented further tragedy. The family accepted this accident as divine intervention. In our lives, I believe that God intervenes to help us but we may not recognize that it's for our own good.

Many people have limits in every area of their life. We need to be open to those amazing possibilities in life. We need to take the limits off of God and off ourselves. If we dwell on the past failures or disappointments then it's more likely that your vision will be impaired to what is possible. If you are dwelling on the past, it's more difficult to live a life of abundance.

"Now unto him that is able to do exceeding abundantly above all that we ask or think, according to the power with workest in us (Ephesians 3:20)." This beautiful declaration of truth of God's unlimited ability to answer prayers is connected to his unique power that works in us. This power inside of is actually the presence of God himself. In Acts 1:8 before Jesus was taken up into heaven, he told His disciples that, "you shall receive power when the Holy Spirit has come upon you..." We have incredible power inside of us waiting to be tapped. This power comes from the Holy Spirit. Our thoughts and our attitudes will allow us to either tap into this power for positive or for the negative. With such a resource of unlimited spiritual power working in us, God is able to accomplish far more than we can ever imagine, as He works in and through those yielded to God will. Because of this infinite potential, we can be filled "with all joy and peace in believing, that you may abound in hope, through the power of the Holy Ghost (Romans 15:13)."

We have an infallible guide, the Bible, as well as other ancient texts of wisdom. Mathew 7:7-8 advises us, "Ask, and it will be given to you; seek, and you will find; knock, and it will be opened to you. For everyone who asks receives, and he who seeks finds, and to him who knocks it will be open." What are you asking for in life?

'Know Better' Life Question: What are your thoughts and words currently bringing into your life? Are you using your thoughts and words to describe your life situation as abundant and limitless?

Your life is as wonderful or as broken as you make it. The old adage which says, "life is what you make it" is true. We draw into our lives what our thoughts dwell on. The concept of karma, sowing and reaping and the law of attraction all state that we can affect the quality of our own lives by the thoughts that we choose to focus on.

2 Timothy 1:7 states, "For God has not given us a spirit of fear, but of power and love and a sound mind." How many of us actually have internalized this verse? I never knew I had the power until I was forced to slow down, look inside myself lovingly and critically in order to make a change. I was brought up in the church but all the words just went in one ear and out the other. How many of you are the same way. I did not know that I had power inside of me or that I mattered outside of my stuff or my job. I matter because God matters. God made me and you, and loves us unconditionally. Hebrew 4:16 states, "Let us come boldly to the throne of grace, that we may obtain mercy and find grace to help us in time of need." God saved my life! God

helped me in my darkest hour of need and is waiting to help you too. All everyone needs to do is to ask, seek and knock!

I mentioned how Paul wrote in Philippians 4:13 that, "I can do all things through Christ, who strengthens me." Power without limits is waiting for you is you can eradicate all negative thought and focus on pure and honest intention. If you break free from the prison of the mind then all things are possible. I changed my nature by being good to myself, changing my inner and outer dialogue, and believing in a world of infinite possibilities.

There is great power in God's promises. "Delight yourself also in the Lord, and He shall give you the desires of your heart (Psalm 37:40)." We need to think of ourselves in the beautiful manner in which God thinks of us. We need to see ourselves as God sees us, with a boundless spirit of power. "Be of good courage, and He shall strengthen your heart, all you who hope in God (Psalm 31:24)."

It comes down to belief; you are what you believe that you are. Being steadfast is vital in this step. You must consistently believe in yourself and the power inside of you. You must have not one strand of doubt or fear. You must have an unwavering belief that God loves you and has a plan for your life. You must understand that God's plan for your life is greater and more abundant than you can imagine. God wants you to succeed and all that you need to do is to align your thoughts, words and actions to those of God and all things are then possible.

"The human body is capable of amazing physical deeds. If we could just free ourselves from our perceived limitations and tap into our internal fire, the possibilities are endless," says Dean Karnazes, ultra-marathoner and best-selling author.

Bruce Lee stated, *"If you always put limits on everything you do, physical or anything else, it will spread into your work and into your life. There are no limits. There are only plateaus, and you must go beyond them."*

C.S. Lewis believed that, *"You are never too old to set another goal or to dream a new dream."*

"It's not about perfection. It's about effort. And when you bring that effort every single day, that's where transformation happens. That's how change occurs." Jillian Michaels

Remember; do not let anyone limit you. You are a rock star! Believe it!

Chapter 7

Step Four: *Work out daily in three areas: physical, mental and spiritual.*

<u>**'Know Better' Life Question:**</u> How does one get it? How does one get to a place of whole and healthy?

Answer: By working out the three areas of our lives.

I think the first word gives us a clue. "HOW" which can be broken down as--H-honesty, O-openness, W-willingness. Honesty, openness and willingness are the start of a different type of relationship one can have with oneself. There is a saying, "you can't find peace if you are living by faulty principles."

Dr. Drew Pinsky in his book *Cracked* says that "*At a certain point, they (those in recovery) just have to want to get it. The light has to go on inside.*" I located my light once I decided to lean on God's understanding and not my own understanding. Proverbs 3:5-6 states, "Trust in the Lord with all your heart, and lean not on your own understanding; in all your ways acknowledge Him, and He shall direct your paths."

People used to believe that the world was flat but after many years and evidence people begin to believe that what they stood on was flat but that the world is round. There were some who still did not believe that world was round because they believed what they saw. The same is still going on today whereby there are some people who still refuse to believe that the world is one of infinite possibilities. These unfortunate people are still seeing the world as flat; seeing their world as flat.

Therapists talk about the importance of cognitively restructuring our thoughts which I believe is so important--critically vital to transforming one's life. That said, it's also important to restructure our physical and spiritual lives in addition to our thoughts.

Honesty may seem like an interesting point to bring up in this section but to be whole and healthy one has to be honest in all areas of one's life. Too many people are not honest with themselves in various areas but it's only through honesty that one can grow beyond old hurts. I heard a saying which said, "We are only as sick as our secrets." Too many people allow the illusions to rule their lives.

My honest moment of clarity was to realize that my physical body was fit but my mind and spirit was unhealthy. My body was in better shape than my mind or spirit, I was out of balance. Self-diagnostic or an honest internal assessment is critical to transform one's life. After being honest, then comes the part dealing with being open. Being open is a challenge for many people because we have invested time, energy and efforts in our current point of view. If your current program (whatever that may be--body, mind or spirit) is not getting you the specific and measurable goals that you want then it's time for a change. You need to be open to a new way of doing things. Drop the ego and ask for help if you need it. Seek and you shall find is a piece of wisdom that Jesus spoke, and it's as true as it was years ago. So, first get honest with yourself and then be open to a new way of doing things. In this age of free information on the internet, there is no reason for anyone to say that they don't know how. Lastly, you have been honest, look at yourself and figure out where you need work without judging yourself (this is a later step but it's important to say this now). You have to develop an open attitude to learn a new way to doing things. Now is where 'the rubber meets the road' as my father always says-willingness. You must be willing to start doing things in a new way now.

One can know that exercise is good for themselves - which is being honest. This same person can be open to exercise being good but until one is willing to exercise, then it can't help you. Many people confuse health and fitness. You can be overweight according to the doctors and be healthy or be within the weight guidelines and be unhealthy. Health is an overall condition of wellness. Health is measured by a healthy lifestyle in all the three areas. For example, you can work out 5 hours a day but if your diet is bad then it can lead to the same health risks that you are trying to avoid. Diet is 70 percent of the equation when trying to be healthy. When I say diet, I mean what you actually eat. I don't mean diet systems like Nutrisystem, Jenny Craig or Weight Watchers. I am against 'organized diets' or diet systems but I support eating in a healthy and balanced fashion. You can be skinny and unhealthy. Maybe that skinny person has a good diet but does not exercise so he/she is in the same unhealthy boat.

Fitness is the ability to undertake physical activity while health deals with the state of all the systems in the body--psychological, muscular, circulatory, digestive, lymphatic, nervous and your spirit. Most people believe that being fit means that you are healthy but this is not necessary the case. We need to train our bodies, minds and spirit for optimal health.

Physical:

Exercise is broken into two categories: Aerobic and anaerobic. Aerobic literally means 'with oxygen' and refers to moderate exercise performed over a period of time. Examples of aerobic exercises are activities such as riding the bike, running, or using the elliptical. While anaerobic literally means 'without oxygen' and refers to exercises that produce short burst of power. Anaerobic exercise burns glycogen as its main fuel while causing the body to store some fat. Anaerobic exercises are strength building exercises such as lifting weights and body weight exercises such as pushups or pulls ups. To ensure complete physical fitness, one should train their metabolism and do both types of exercise. All exercise requires a person to build an aerobic foundation. By properly developing your aerobic foundation, you will increase your overall health, burn off extra fat, improve your thinking and immune system, allowing you to sleep better and provide you with more energy. Once you train your metabolism, your body will begin to help you to maintain better fitness.

There are many ways to exercise. As everyone always hear, please consult a doctor before starting an exercise routine. Once you get a doctor's approval then start slow such as a walking routine. You should walk with purpose and effort so that your breathing is steady and not labored for 30 minutes several times a week. Over time, you can increase your pace and effort so that you will move into the aerobic zone. Aerobic activity increases the health of your heart while will increase the quality of your life over time. Experts say that we should do 150 minutes a week of aerobic activity a week for optimal health.

Here is one trap that people who start to exercise fall into. They work out for an hour but will then go to work or home and sit the rest the day. That hour will not counteract the sedentary lifestyle that you are engaged in the rest of the day especially if your diet is still bad. What I suggest is to get up every hour and walk for a few minutes such as walking down the stairs or around the building. This helps to get the blood moving and keeps the mind active as well. It's all about moving. For example, at home you can keep your metabolism moving by standing up and pacing in place during the commercials while watching your TV show. Exercise is life and moving will allow your metabolism to continue to be active throughout the day.

Re diet, there are many diet plans out there. I like to keep things simple. Eat more fruits and vegetables and less processed food. Eat things with color and avoid eating things white such as white rice or white potatoes or white bread. Eat less carbohydrates (carbs) overall. Carbs create that unhealthy belly fat that is very dangerous as we all get older. If you can keep our carb intake under 100 grams a day and are exercising then we will lose weight. If you want to maintain your weight then keep your carbs around 100-150 grams a day while exercising. I am not providing comprehensive information on diets or fitness but just an introduction to those who are looking for a place to start. If you start a daily routine of moving (exercise) and continue it while monitoring what you eat then you will become healthier.

Mental:

There is an old Buddhist scripture which begins, "*Our life is shaped by our mind; we become what we think.*" In Proverbs 23:7, it states, "for as a man thinks in his heart, so as he is." Just as we train our body, training our mind is important to optimal health. Our mind is the results of our past thinking. Too many people live in bad neighborhoods of the mind as I mentioned earlier. These people constantly visit old traumas and past hurts. It's time to move beyond those hurts. This is done by training our mind to focus on elevated and inspired thoughts. The more you return to those bad neighborhoods of the mind (past hurts, pain, grudges, unforgiveness, traumas, fears, doubts and the like) it becomes the default setting in your mind which prevents you from achieving greatness. When those thoughts come up through memories, you need to change the channel in your mind. You have the power, no one forces you to return to those past hurts. No one, except yourself, forces you to relive those mental traumas. Please give yourself a break, treat yourself better and more gently.

Many people live in the past or future as opposed to living in the present moment. You can become free once you allow yourself to be mindful of the present moment. Living in the present moment is liberating and allows you to become truly alive. So many people are waiting for something while never enjoying life as it goes by.

I started taking yoga as a way to relax because I was in a bad neighborhood mentally. While yoga has gained popularity over the years, I was hesitant because I thought it was connected with the religion and/or not physically challenging. I was wrong on both accounts because it can be physically challenging and does not have to be connected to any specific religion.

As stated in the Yoga Sutras, "Yoga is the settling of the mind into silence. When the mind has settled, we are established in our essential nature, which is unbound consciousness." I realized this to be very intriguing so I went into it with an open mind. I found that yoga was able to get me beyond the ego's identification with the mind and body, and it gives us a direct connection with our true spiritual self. Yoga was about getting to know oneself. I learned how to breathe and it led me to a better meditative practice. Breathing is a form of meditation and can lead to finding inner stillness.

Psalms 47:10 states, "Be still and know that I am God." It was difficult for me to know God when I was always moving in the past. Abdominal Breathing is an important part of becoming fully conscious and transforming our lives. At the end of my yoga session, we would clasp our hands together and say Namaste which translated to "the light in me recognizes the light in you". I became convinced of the physical and mental benefits of yoga and I would recommend anyone who wants to be good to themselves. I became more balanced and centered. It was from yoga I stared to become more mindful during the day. I now understand through my meditation practices, from looking inward and being self-aware that change is possible.

Avoid thoughts of a more base level. The prolonged habit of focusing on negative thoughts has harmful, negative effects on our physical health. It is well established medical fact between the correlation of negative mental thought patterns and some physical maladies such as high blood pressure, digestive disturbances and other medical issues. On the other hand, those individuals who focus on uplifting and positive thoughts often have better health. Too many people are driven by their demons: need to be accepted, need to be perfect, need to be successful/rich or famous.

Meditation is one of the best ways to exercise the mind. Allow your mind to be quiet. Psalm 46:10 states, "Be still and know that I am God." Allowing the mind to be still has more recuperative powers than actual sleep at times. You can train your mind to not go to those bad neighborhoods if you stop allowing your thoughts to run wild. You have the power to change your life by changing your thoughts. There are many ways to develop a meditative practice. The Buddhists offer much in terms of learning how to retrain the mind through meditation. The next chapter delves into prayer and meditation.

Exercising the mind also is done through learning or practicing a foreign language, playing scrabble, doing crossword puzzles or Sudoku. One can also exercise the mind by learning a new skill or writing. If you do something that you are passionate about when exercising the mind, the benefits will be enormous.

Spiritual:

In order to move from unhealthy habits to a whole and healthy lifestyle, we must understand what has previously driven us (honesty again) and realign ourselves with a daily spiritual practice. We hold the creative power of the universe within us but it you are living a defective or broken life; you will not be able to tap into that power until you start to think different by moving closer to God. That power is from God and it's centered in loved. We can recover and heal ourselves by starting an ambitious program of spiritual growth.

Most people do not have a deep and daily spiritual practice. These people may pray nightly and may go to church regularly but their spiritual practice is not deep. Their prayer life is not deep. They still live in a state of willful sin. The lifestyle of a true believer should be apparent to all but too many people hate too much and love too little. God's tools are love, forgiveness, kindness, generosity, worship, long suffering, faith and belief. These traits need to be the center of a spiritual practice. Be honest with God, open with God and willing to be obedient and watch doors opens up of inner peace and joy. The Bible says that we shall be known by the fruits of our labors. We can recover when we connect our lives with the guidance of the Bible. The purpose of all major religious traditions is to help us cope with life's uncertainties and build good qualities in us.

'Know Better' Life Question: Is your current spiritual practice working for you? Do you need more Jesus?

There is a song by Erica Campbell called '*A little More Jesus*' where she sings "I need a little more Jesus, to help me along my way." I love this song because it always encourages me. If you are a little discouraged, play the song and I guarantee that you will be lifted up.

Chapter 6

Prayer and Meditation

We are going to take a brief intermission from the steps to focus on an important part of empowering ourselves. Prayer and meditation are important aspects of most spiritual traditions and it allows us to take our destiny into our own hands. Prayer is powerful as it directs our consciousness to God. Through prayer, we request assistance from God. Prayer is worthwhile because takes us outside of ourselves and directs us to Him. Prayer encourages humility and brings guidance. Prayer can help release tension, anxiety and stress. Prayer can lead to healing and a better understanding of the divine nature. Prayer is about communicating with God, speaking and listening. Prayer involves hope and faith. Prayer is energy. Hope is positive energy. Faith is positive energy. When we connect right prayer with hope and faith, we open up a creative force into our lives which can be powerful in fulfilling our dreams.

The urge to pray is universal. Around the whole world and in every culture, everyone prays. People pray when they are happy, sad, confused, upset and through every other emotion. Energy is a concept I never understood before but through prayer and meditation I started to understand how my actions contributed to my mood, emotions and my overall well-being. It's through the channeling of the positive energy of prayer that we can thrive and live an abundant life in a sea of chaos and despair.

The spiritual life is oriented toward God. Man rebels against himself because life is well worth living but man must believe this and make conscious decisions toward life. There is that great commandment that Jesus tells us about Loving God first and then loving our neighbor as ourselves. After loving God, we must, must love ourselves first. We should all live a life which shows that we truly love ourselves. Life has meaning and our purpose is to discover this meaning. Prayer and meditation will allow us to discover our meaning and purpose. Life strives to keep us bound to illusions and delusions. Finding ourselves is the goal. Its only through prayer and meditation that one can learn one's true nature.

Prayer is energy and we need to make sure that our prayers should be in line with God's word. I had to learn how to pray, making sure that I pray for the right things. I learned that some things I was praying for was in my power to change, not God's, because God had already done his part and gave me what I needed. I just had to look inside to activate the power that God had already given me. Right prayer is hope, hope for a better life. Hope and Faith are both so important to elevating one's life. My conversion was not like Paul's on the road to Damascus because it was a process over a decade. Coming to the Savior was a long process for me. Many people, like me, may need time and multiple exposures to the Gospel before they are ready to make a decision.

Even if God has predisposed things in a certain way, we can still change our course because, as it says in 1 John 3:2, "we are children of God." The relationship between us as the created and God as the Creator is one where we have within us the breath of God. There is no higher positive energy than the breath of God. We are connected to God, prayer and meditation allows us to bridge that gap between the Creator and the created. What we call the will of God is intrinsically linked to our will. If our will is weak then our life will be one of defeat and weakness but if we understand whose we are and what was entered into us, then we can achieve what God wants for us.

I want to interject for one moment. Faith in Christ does not make us immune to spiritual weariness or faithlessness of heart. This condition may arise from the frustrations in the world but we must not be swayed by what the devil is trying to do. We must understand the traps that the devil is placing out there. We must remember who we are. We are empowered by the Holy Spirit so when you feel weak, you can rely on God to help us. Being a Christian gives us something to hold us up when we feel weary.

There was an anonymous poem I came to love.

"When the trials of this life make you weary, and your troubles seem too much to bear,

There's a wonderful solace and comfort, in the silent communion of prayer."

Many people speak to God during prayer but we should also strive to listen during prayer. During the listening part of prayer is when we can move to meditation. We can meditate on a specific scripture in an effort to hear His voice. This type of meditation is an important facet of worship. Also, along this same path is mindful meditation, which can be restorative. Any type of meditation can be a gateway which can lead us to God. In meditation, we discover basic goodness and practical relaxation. I equate being awake with not sleepwalking through life or walking around without awareness. Sleep is what happens when people either forget or ignore basic goodness. When we act on guilt, fear and insecurity then people are able to do horrendous things.

'Know Better' Life Principle: **Don't allow anyone to steal your happiness. We have the power to not be affected by our outer circumstances.**

Once we decide to work on our inside, the outside becomes less of a problem. I learned through prayer and meditation that peace, love and happiness had to begin inside before I could offer it to anyone else. I realized that when I took care of myself, I was able to add a little bit of goodness into the world. There is so much pain, anger, suffering, fear, worry and anxiety in the world today that when we take care of these feelings, we improve the world around us. When we take care of ourselves by being healthier, more loving and gentle; the world around us recognizes that something good has occurred. We can be a beacon for others because when people see that we have lifted ourselves out of the muck then they realize that they can lift themselves up to.

How to pray: We pray with our minds, our words and our bodies. Every action we do can be a part of prayer if we are mindful. The Buddhists call meditation 'being mindful or watching our thoughts' but I find that when I pray correctly I am also watching my thoughts and being mindful. Having a God-consciousness is about being mindful of our thoughts, words and actions. Understanding, compassion, love, forgiveness, all requires mindfulness in this world in its current state. When I channel those positive forces, the corresponding energy provides a better world for all those around me. In prayer, the electric current is love. To pray correctly, our body and mind must be at a point of peace infused with love. We should pray that we see the world as God sees the world. If we change the way we view the world (seeing the world with love and compassion) then things will no longer bother us. Every day when I see people being cruel, I pray for them. I have grown to love those around me even the unlovable. We must have compassion and pray for those who are still trapped in fear, anger and other negative states. I strived to be a beacon for those who were still lost. You can strive to be a beacon to others too.

When I decided to live (and it was a conscious decision), I realized that I had always been a seeker and now I am seeking to know more of the mind of God. I fully support all religious and spiritual traditions although I am a follower of Christ. Genghis Khan stated, "Just as there are five fingers leading to the hand, there are many different paths to salvation." I read that quote and made a commitment to never be a spiritual coward. I decided to look at other parallel spiritual traditions in order to have a richer experience in my tradition. I wanted to focus on prayer and meditation as it's a central part of Christianity, and thought I would look at Buddhism as a way to look into meditation. When I started reading Buddhist literature, I learned that from the Buddha's teaching, they believe that true happiness is found within. As I looked at Christian scripture and saw that this was parallel to what the Apostle Paul wrote in 1st Corinthians 3:16, "Do you not know that you are the temple of God and that the Spirit of God dwells within you." I started understanding that so many people had the bad habit of looking for happiness in transient experiences instead of looking inside. Through the conditioning that I had discussed when the illusion falls away, our original mind is revealed.

Meditation can lead to revealing that original mind. Through life, we are conditioned and programmed as discussed in Part I. From this programming, we get further and further from who we were born to be. But through mindfulness and watching our minds we can do something different in order to return back to that original mind which elevated ourselves.

Psalms 1:1-2 states, "Blessed is the man who walks not in the counsel of the ungodly, nor stands in the path of sinners, nor sits in the seat of the scornful; but his delight is in the law of the Lord, and in His law he meditates day and night."

A meditative practice gives us time to slow down and wake up to the naturally occurring love in our hearts. Meditation is self-reflection without judgment. We embrace our feelings of the present moment. Depth and insight can only occur when we are present in the moment. The ancient ones who meditated learned that humans need a period of seeming inactivity to make a measurable growth or change. When we allow ourselves to watch our thoughts and feelings, we take the opportunity to tune into the present moment. Life is richer when we learn to relish the present moment; not yearning for some future moment or regretting/worrying about some past experience.

Meditation is a very personal experience. I can describe how meditation is important in becoming more aware and I can explain how to begin a meditative practice but it's up to you to make that commit to your well-being. Even if you meditate five minutes daily, it allows our mind to do nothing. It's resting without the ego which is empowering. Meditation can allow us to transform our suffering into a rescue boat of mercy. It's only through meditation that we can look directly at our own mind and discover its true nature. I realized that I could find clarity when things around me were in chaos. Change happens in life, we have to make peace with it.

We can open up our hearts if we look inwards. Opening up our hearts allows us to transform into a state of being more peaceful, loving and understanding. Meditation is a relaxation practice. I know that I was at first hesitant but once I realized what it was, I embraced it. Meditation allows us to become closer to God because it creates less interference in our minds, which can get in the way with our spiritual practice. You can practice relaxation breathing sitting or lying down by breathing deeply into the stomach. Deep meditative relaxation practices allow us to shake off the tension of daily life. We can walk freer when we are taking care of our minds. When I reduced the tension, I felt lighter and the inner pain was reduced.

I learned that Zen masters of meditation can change their brain waves. We all can do the same if we work to master our own minds. The human brain and its consciousness contain so many mysteries. In order to raise our consciousness we must prep the battlefield, our mind. We must free ourselves from the conditioning of the past. To escape the prison of the mind by winning the war inside, the collection of information is vital. We must begin by collecting information for the battle, prayer and meditation can help us in this operation. We must love ourselves enough to look inside. It okay, there is nothing in your mind that is not in anyone else's mind.

The brain is such an important part of us, a fifth of our blood is used for supplying the brain. It's the hard drive of our computer. We have to prepare the battlefield for the change which will take place. We begin by being mindful; thinking good, clean, pure, happy, non-harmful, abundant thoughts for ourselves and others. I stopped thinking bad thoughts of others (which was hard for me at first) and then transitioned into thinking good and abundant thoughts for everyone even those who wished me harm. This was the first step in aligning my thoughts with those of God's.

Preparing our minds for the transition to a higher state requires an intention to do so. When I decided to raise my consciousness, I started meditating on the process. I begin visualizing myself changing. I started challenging myself and my beliefs. I basically told myself that change was coming and that it was easy. I kept saying this mantra throughout the day when I felt at my lowest. I was preparing myself for the change. I was preparing myself to reverse my conditioning and socialization, training and experience from the world. I knew that I had a big fight ahead of myself. The brain's cerebral cortex is the home for higher functions; reason and creative thinking that separates us from lower forms of animals. The cerebral cortex is where we process the information necessary to operate in the world. The brain constantly rewires itself to become an organ different than what it was previously. The brain never rests because it's always working, processing new experiences and discarding old experiences. The brain does not get enough rest when sleeping.

The Bible discusses man's experiences with God, how to live and the power within us. It's important to read the Bible as a way to be closer to God. To me, the bible was daunting and distant but prayer and meditation opened up the enthusiasm to begin a meaningful spiritual practice. I love the word 'enthusiasm' because it comes from the Greek word meaning to be inspired or possesses by God according to Webster's dictionary. Passion and enthusiasm is important in life, an inner fire. We all need to have an inner fire for God just as we have for our favorite sports team or our favorite activity. We need to be like an inner light seeking its own source. I say this because it's about looking within to our divine nature. In meditation, we are able to get closer to this inner fire which allows us to have more meaning in our lives.

I remember when I first tried meditation not related to focusing on God's word but quieting my mind. I was trying to make my mind become quiet and had problems focusing. I asked my Yoga teacher if he had any suggestions and he advised me to allow my mind to become still. He explained that I should not force my mind to become still but too allow it to become still or quiet. Meditation is about harnessing our thoughts in order to retrain own minds. I had to maintain determined patience and daily practice. If we take as little as 10 minutes a day meditating, the benefits will be exponential. I had problems stilling my mind, body and spirit but through practice I was able to eventually go up to 20 minutes a day. 20 minutes a day is optimal in the practice. Even after succeeding to some extent there were days where it more difficult than others. I found that stilling my mind allowed me to get closer to the spiritual core. I would at times focus on my desire to become closer to His will, His way and His Spirit becoming my way.

I would often meditate before praying because the Bible tells us to not approach the alter of God if we have anything against our neighbor. Meditating would center me and allow a peace come over me before I prayed. I found that meditation increased my ability to focus and I felt healthier. I want to stress that meditation does not lessen the need for prayer because it does not take the place of prayer. Meditation in conjugation with prayer can allow us to better hear God's voice. Mastering the technique of meditation is not easy and it takes constant practice. I wanted to change my nature and realized this after studying the nature of my mind through meditation. I had to first keep track of what my mind was doing and how my mind was doing it which I did through meditation. Once I knew what was happening, I was automatically able to gain better control over my uncontrolled thoughts.

I believe that the only way to change is to change our thinking. The brain has about 100 million neurons with each linking with each other so that the entire network makes up the most complicated object in the universe. Both the brain and the body need exercise in order to stay healthy. The brain works better when the body is healthy. So, once I became physically healthier than my mental functions began to improve too. I found the more I focused on being good and gentle with myself, the more I felt better. We all have the seeds for our own happiness inside of us. Prayer and meditation allow us to find those seeds.

Neuroscientists have determined that joy or happiness seems to be more nature than nurture. These scientists believe that 60 percent of an individual's tendency to have a character dominated by positive emotions comes from his/her genetic makeup. The rest is learned through experiences, emotions, and thoughts. Now some may read this information and say that joy or happiness is out of their hands but I read this and understand that it confirms that we have the power in us. We are able to choose 40 percent of our basic happiness. I knew that if I started pouring inside of me good things such as spiritual wisdom, thoughts or readings then I could affect my inner mood positively. When I started watching my thoughts and became more mindful of everything I did, I realized that I was no longer as affected the things around me. It was about me and my development. It's all about each one of us harnessing the intention to change then make a plan to put it into action.

This consciousness was so important to my overall well-being. I soon discovered that putting on frowns and smiles each had a dramatic effect on my mood. Psychiatrists say that bad news sticks longer than good news, as well as unpleasant encounters affect the brain more powerfully than pleasant ones. Negative feelings such as sadness, fear, worry, anxiety affect the brain more powerfully than positive feeling such as love, compassion, etc. I also found that bad moods stick longer than good moods but that I had the power to modify my moods by smiling or thinking good thoughts or visualizing something good. I learned through the practice of meditation that I could gain more control over my mind.

Psychologists explain that fear activates the autonomic system and releases stress hormones, including adrenaline. Anger, like fear, manifests itself through a variety of pathways in the brain starting with the limbic system. Anger releases cortisol in the brain which increases levels of stress and frustration. These emotions are a defense mechanism for when we were cave people and needed a "fight or flight" response in order to survive. Psychologists also say that habitually angry people appear to have reduced neural activity in their frontal lobes, which communicate with the amygdala as the mind seeks balance between reason and emotion. I found from personal experience that all my negative feelings took everything out of me and no matter what anyone said did anything to help me until I decided to turn the switch on inside of me by learning how my mind worked and how I had the power. Yoda stated in Star Wars, "*Named must your fear, before banish it you can.*" Even though this quote is from a movie, the wisdom rings true. Just as Yoda also stated, "*You must unlearn what you have learned.*" We must all unlearn those unhealthy habits in order to allow the light to come in.

I found out that scientists also stated that people with depression felt the worse in the morning. I started to wake up with prayer and meditation to improve my mood. I focused on changing the feelings and visualized turning my internal switch to happiness and joy. I also used positive self-talk to move beyond those feelings of depression.

Meditation is the center of Buddhist practice. I learned that I could learn a lot from how the Buddhist sought to become more mindful through meditation. The Buddhists believe that reality can be found in the present moment. It's through meditation that the practitioner arrives at a deep understanding of reality. Being in the present moment has the great ability to liberate us from fear, worry, anxiety and sadness. Being in the moment and understanding that we can only find true happiness in the here and now is an important concept to grasp to live an abundant life. When one meditates and starts to become more mindful, the quality of one's life will improve which will bring about more peace and freedom.

We do not have to go to church, a temple, a mosque or any other place of worship to practice meditation because it can be done at home or at work. Meditation can nourish and heal the body and mind. We put so much stress and worry on our minds that it's only when we sleep that our minds get any sort of relief. Even now in today's society, people do not detach from the world. Some people sleep with their Smartphone in order to respond to the external. Meditation is about looking inward to the source, God. In daily life, our minds have the tendency to worry about the future or feel bad about the past. Meditation will allow us to bring our thoughts back to the present. The present is where life is taking place. The present offers so much richness and glory. We can only connect to God in the present. The Lord's Prayer in the Bible tells us to ask God to provide us our daily bread. We ask for this day, not for tomorrow. "Give us this day, our daily bread." I think this line is about being in the moment, in a positive and healthy manner.

I studied how many religious traditions pray and learned that there was times when I was praying for the wrong things, not all my prayers were in line with God's intention. I begin to figure out a better way to pray because I came to believe that it was only through prayer and meditation that my life could evolve to a higher level. I found seven principles which would help to make prayer more effective:

> *1-Expressing thanks for our faith and for the change which knowing God has produced in our lives. My life was changed through knowing God (God-Consciousness).*

> *2-Asking God to help us to know what He wants us to do for Him (our purpose).*

> *3-Asking God for deep spiritual understanding (wisdom).*

> *4-Asking God to help us to live for Him (meaning).*

> *5-Asking God to give us more knowledge of His nature.*

6-Asking God to give us strength to endure (endurance to live in this fallen world without being conformed).

7-Asking God to fill us with joy, strength and thankfulness each day.

In reading the New Testament, we read that we are of God. In Buddhism, the practitioners believe that the one they are praying to lies inside as well as outside of them. The Buddhists believe that it's a mistake to believe God is only on the outside. In Christianity, we have a divine spark inside of us and God is with us. It's like a reinforcement process; God is within us and around us. Isaiah 41:10 states, "Fear not, for I am with you; be not dismayed, for I am your God. I will strengthen you, yes, I will help you, I will uphold you with My righteous right hand." Three verses later in Isaiah 41:13, we also learn, "For I, the Lord your God, will hold your right hand, Saying to you, 'Fear not, I will help you." There are parallel paths in so many of the world religions. When we see that the light is in us, around us and above us, we can achieve a level of abundance heretofore not realized. God wants us to be happy and live an abundant life, why not align our desires up with what God wants for us?

Prayer and meditation allow us to become closer to the divine nature in each of us. Ephesians 5:14 states, "Awake, you who are sleep, arise from the dead, and Christ will give you light." We must all wake up from the sleep which has covered out eyes for so long. Waking up and living in the present is one of the keys to happiness. The Buddha taught, "*the past is already gone and the future has not yet come. Life can only be touched in the present moment. In the spirit of meditation, life can only be touched in the here and now.*"

We help ourselves to be whole and healthy when we live in the present. I suffered from depression at one point in my life and I was able to use mindfulness to look after my own issues and to bring my mind into contact with the conditions needed for relief. My practice of mindfulness of my thoughts and feelings helped me to recognize my thoughts and feeling in the moment. Once I could separate the various thoughts and feelings, I was able to move slowly forward and get closer to God. I came to the realization that no one was coming to save me, I would have to actively participate in my own rescue. Through meditation, I was able to recognize the source of my feelings in those moments when I was watching my thoughts. I found that I could have joy and peace in the present moment through following a simple plan:

-Prayer first thing in the morning and throughout the day.

-Seek spiritual wisdom every day where ever I can find it. I decided that it was about filling my internal cup each day with good, wholesome and pure energy each day.

-Meditate on God's word. Meditate on my thoughts, being mindful.

-Think good thoughts, speak good words and do good all day long.

-Help others daily

-Work out daily

-Be the light for others

-Show kindness to myself and to others

-Be grateful every moment of the day

I discovered that when I created a simple life plan my life became easier. I realized that there are pathways in the brain which become used to being utilized. The brain takes you quickly to places you need to go but the brain can also take you to places you do not want to go like sadness, depression, jealousy and anger. Through training, I was able to use the power of my mind to retrain the pathways in my brain. We can all do this by becoming more mindful of our thoughts.

Practical methods to meditate.

It's easy and so simple that I wished I had started a meditative practice years before. The key I had to do was to commit to a daily practice. To start, begin with intention. Tell yourself that I plan to allow my mind to become still. Cut off the phone, TV and everything else that may disturb your practice. Just sit down or lay down (I prefer to sit) and relax. If you are sitting, straighten your back. Sit with purpose at the edge of the chair. Your posture should be upright with your hands on your knees. Next, I would focus on becoming more aware of my breath. Listen to where your breath is going; it's probably going in your chest as most people breathe too shallowly. Focus on your breathing. Follow your breath, paying attention to the air as it goes in and out. Pay attention to you out breath. After following your natural breath, start to breath in the stomach. This is conscious breath.

Begin breathing long deep breaths into and out of the stomach. Feel your stomach rise and fall with each breath. Count one when you breathe in and count two when you exhale. Take long breaths and continue to count with each breath to ten and then start over. When you are meditating, all kinds of things will come into your mind, conversations with your boss, plans for the future, details about you marriage and other thoughts. All kinds of things will enter your mind. Let the thoughts come and go, do not dwell on the thoughts. Do not judge the thoughts. Do not label the thoughts as good or bad. Just watch your thoughts as they go back, trying to allow your mind to become quiet. By letting your thoughts come and go you will begin to retrain your mind. The goal is to eventually allow your mind to become still. Our minds have so much traffics going in and out that it will take daily practice to recondition our minds to start to quiet. Aloneness is the point, being alone with your thoughts without judging or labeling. This deliberate practice will allow you to become more aware. By focusing on watching your thoughts, you create new pathways for your thoughts. These new pathways will produce immediate benefits in giving you more composure and attentiveness. You will discover a deeper form of relaxation by practicing to quiet your mind.

Researchers at Mass General Hospital took Magnetic resonance (MR) brain images of 16 subjects before and after they took a mindfulness-based stress reduction program. MR brain images were also taken of a control group who did not meditate. According to Psychiatry research: Neuroimaging, brain imagery after meditation program showed increase gray-matter density in the hippocampus, important for learning and memory, and in structures associated with self-awareness, compassion and introspection. Lower stress levels correlated with decreased gray-matter density in the amygdala, which plays a role in anxiety and stress. These changes were not seen in the control group.

In a Wake Forest University study, 15 volunteers who had never meditated before attended four 20 minute meditation sessions. Participants' brain activity while a pain-inducing heat device was placed on their leg was examined before and after meditation training. Subjects reported a 40 percent reduction in pain intensity and 57 percent reduction in the unpleasantness of their pain. Morphine typically reduces pain ratings by about 25 percent according to the Journal of Neuroscience. Long term meditation practice can reduce brain atrophy and help dementia. In another study explained in NeuroImage, using Diffusion Tensor Imaging, researchers at UCLA studied 27 active long term meditation practitioners and 27 control subjects. The study found that the meditator's brains showed a range of brain areas with stronger neural connections and less atrophy then those who did not meditate. (Shambhala Sun March 2012).

The Buddhists say that meditation is particularly helpful with internal knots and identity complexes. The Buddhists call the internal knots a collection of delusions, repression, fear and anxiety which have been tied to the depths of our consciousness. They call the 10 chief internal knots: greed, hatred, ignorance, conceit, suspicion, attachment to the body as self, extreme views and prejudices; clinging to rites and rituals; our craving for immortality; and our craving to keep everything just as it is. Our health and our happiness depend on a great extent to transform these ten areas. Pride is considered one of the worse aspects of ourselves in Buddhism and in Christianity as well. Pride led Lucifer to be cast out of heaven. According to Buddhist, suffering arises from anger, jealousy, hatred and shame. So many of us seek solace or joy through consumption. We believe that giving into to our base desires will allow us to forget. Alcohol, drugs or other external vices will not fill that void inside other than God. Too many of us do not want to face what is inside of us. But it's only through looking inward can we heal ourselves and elevate our lives. We draw a lot of negative energy into ourselves each day. Cultivating the energy of mindfulness can help to bring in positive energy to us. The daily practice of watching our thoughts will help us recognize, embrace and transform our feelings of suffering. When we practice mindfulness we do not take sides or judge our thoughts or without craving or without despising the thought. With mindfulness, we simply recognize the sensation we are feeling or thinking.

The pursuit of objects such as money, fame, power, sex cannot produce happiness. We create such agony for ourselves, when the single-minded pursuit of those objects are which we believe are the benchmarks for happiness for us. We humans are all full of desires and we chase after

48

those desires every day. This pursuit makes it difficult to live a wholesome life. The fewer desires we have allow us to live more deeply in the moment. Through meditation, we can lead a more satisfying life, being fully conscious in the present moment.

Being present also means that we must be spiritually alert, not being ignorant of the devils devices, tricks and traps. I started to look at it as what I would do if Jesus was beside me. I had to ask myself if I was doing what was pleasing to God each day realizing that whatever I did was known to God.

My mind is the battlefield and I am a warrior seeking to do what is pleasing to God in order to serve Him. The first line of defense is my thoughts. I have to be diligent in what I think and be careful what I put into my mind. The devil is the adversary and wants to keep me and all of us from going to heaven. When I searched myself I learned that the devil had gained a strong foothold in my mind through years of conditioning. I used to entertain such base and defeating thoughts. These thoughts dragged my spirit down. Our minds were made for good. When we use it for good; good thoughts, good words and good deeds then everything else falls into place. When we allow evil thoughts or any negative thought to enter our mind, we are not doing what is pleasing to God, but what is pleasing for the evil one, satan.

"Do not dwell in the past, do not dream of the future, concentrate the mind on the present moment." Buddha

"Be happy in the moment, that's enough. Each moment is all we need, not more." Mother Teresa

"Mindfulness is simply being aware of what is happening right now without wishing it were different. Enjoying the pleasant without holding on when it changes (which it will). Being with the unpleasant without fearing it will always be this way (which it won't)." James Baraz

Now, let us get back to the next step in the empowerment and love process.

Chapter 7

Step Five: *Be positive always. Say only positive words to others and especially to yourself. Eliminate all negativity and negative people in your lives.*

"A man is happy so long as he chooses to be happy." A. Solzhenitsyn

Being positive is its own reward because we sow what we reap. Some call it 'the law of cause and effect' or 'the law of attraction' or 'karma' but we get back what we put out each day. If we are negative then we draw more negative into our lives. If we are positive then we draw in more positivity into our lives. Every thought, word and action is a seed we plant in the world. All of our lives, we harvest those seeds (and the fruits of those seeds). If we plant lust, greed, covertness, doubt, fear and the like then that is what our lives will be filled with. If we plant positive feelings and emotions like love, understanding, forgiveness, good humor and the like then that is what will return to us.

In the Gospel of Luke, Jesus says, "A good man out of the good treasure of his heart brings forth good; and an evil man out of the evil treasure of his heart brings forth evil. For out of the abundance of the heart his mouth speaks." In Ephesians 4:39, we learn, "Let no corrupt word proceed out of your mouth, but what is good for necessary edification, that it may impart grace to the hearers."

"Go confidently in the direction of your dreams." Henry David Thoreau.

We can only go in the direction of our dreams if we are positive. Positive energy moves us to a place closer to God. God has a purpose and a destiny for everyone's life. If you do not know your purpose, cry out to God to direct you towards your dreams. Being positive helps you achieve your goals. Tell yourself each day, "I can make it," or "I can thrive regardless of the circumstances I find myself in." These phrases of affirmation will help you move towards your aim.

Wisdom and joy comes only from learning how to see a wider, more wondrous world; power comes only from the spirit within. Most of the time we don't use more than a fraction of the spiritual power inside of ourselves. Being positive helps us to harness that inner power. Focus as you go about you daily life trying to live spiritual in the moment. If we focus on our blessings then being positive is so much easier.

I try to say thank you one hundred times a day and it makes me feel better. I thank God for all he had given me. I thanked God for everyone in my life, those who love me or hate me. I asked God to draw all of them closer to Him as he had brought me closer to Him.

"Believing and expecting" is about being positive. God allows us to change the inner narrative. The Bible says that we walk by faith, not sight. Taking a step of faith requires us to be positive. James 5:7 states that we should, "Be patient as you wait." Wait with expectancy while maintaining a positive mental attitude. We have to put the right thoughts and words behind our faith. Believe that God is answering your prayers. Every day that your dream does not come to fruition, is one day closer you are to your dreams. That said, you must do your part and prepare for success. Don't allow any negative word or thought to gain a foothold. Reject any thought that is not of God. Words and thoughts have such creative power. "My best days are ahead of me."

We have a choice in how we choose to see the world. We can see the world as a positive and wondrous place or as a scary and fearful place. Being loving and positive opens a brighter world to all of us. Fear cuts us off from God's inspiration. Do not be afraid to have faith. Fear is negative and a favorite tool of Satan.

Today I live differently. I smile and have a positive, kind word for everyone including those who were all negative. I have eliminated all belittling, limiting thoughts and words from my internal hard drive. The quality of my life improved greatly once I started being more positive. We all have to recreate the internal photo of ourselves in order to change.

Please do not invalidate yourself by putting yourself in a prison of your own making. I learned that the only blueprint in life was the one we make up for ourselves. Life gives us broad strokes to paint the portrait of our lives. Too many people are living broken lives and infecting others with their negativity. You have to decide to end the circle of brokenness.

"The problem is not the problem. The problem is your attitude about the problem." Capt Jack Sparrow

Many of us have built walls between us and God. I did this until I realized that there was a better and more joyous way to live. Many people are mad at God for one reason or another such as abuse, unfairness, incarceration, death of a loved one, foreclosure, bankruptcy, and other issues. They see the world as unfair, not willing to see the lessons that God is trying to teach them in life. I believe that we will continue to encounter the same problems until the problem ceases to bother us. Until we learn the lesson, it will continue to be presented to us. We must understand that everything we are going through is preparing us for a better future. If we are not challenged then we will never grow.

'Know Better' Life Principle: **Every struggle is getting us ready for a higher level of attainment.**

"Our greatest glory is not in never failing, but in rising up every time we fail." Ralph Waldo Emerson

Too many people are addicted to their pain. Too many people are addicted to their anger. Too many people are addicted to having negativity inside of them. If one draws closer to God, then God will draw closer to them. This statement is echoed in the Holy Qur'an and the Bible in James 4:8. We draw closer to God by changing our identity as our identity has been connected to our jobs, loved ones, material objects but those things cannot lead to being internally content.

How to bring elements of peace into your life? Look deeply inside and see the truth; accept it and then more on to a better, more positive place. God is about love, a positive force. Look inward and make a change on the inside.

We all have the power to change our own lives inside of us. We must be steadfast and unmovable to activate this power. What I mean is that you can change with the wind when something negative comes in your live or you can say that you will not give up. You must be steadfast in your attitude. The devil loves inconsistency. To activate this internal power in your life, you must remove the walls between you and God. Removing that wall or any other impediment between you and God will allow you to recreate your future in a way you want it. Those good breaks and blessings will start to appear out of nowhere once you train your mind to be consistently positive. Our beliefs create our world view which in turn leads to our actions.

'Know Better' Life Question: How does one start to live a more positive life?

We start the process of moving forward by releasing the past. Free yourself from negative thoughts/acts. Forgive and do not bring it up again. Forgive and then love that person with all your heart--they are just as broken as we are but when we become more enlightened, we can move beyond the hurts. I forgave all those who ever done me wrong and started praying that God would bless them. When I did this, I changed on the inside-I was free. Many of us have had people who have hurt but if you want to reach your full potential, then you must move beyond those traumas of the past.

We can free ourselves from all that junk. Drama creates pain. Attend to your pain and hurts. If you cut yourself badly on your arm, you would get administer treatment to that wound. It is the same with your internal wounds. Your body has an inner energy field which you can tap into through positivity. The first step is to surrender completely to God. God is love and forgiveness is a commandment. Love, compassion and seeing life for the amazing gift that it is everyday helps us to move on.

It's an unfortunate certainty in life that pain comes in everyone's life at one time or another. How does one get beyond that pain? I learned that I had to integrate my pain and then strive to move on. I learned how to see the positive in my experiences and not to dwell on the negative. The only way to move forward is to move through the pain, not around it. You may never get over it but you get used to it. Moving on is a part of life. Many people can never get beyond the hurt or betrayal of that loved one leaving. We can all take that tragic thing that happened to us and turn it into something meaningful and purposeful. We can honor the memory of that loved one or work harder to not be what the detractors say about us. Every day we have a choice, we can do the same old things that we have done or we can be better.

Cicero said, "Any man may make a mistake; none but a fool will persist in it." Cast off the baggage of the past and push yourself to be disciplined in staying positive despite the outer circumstances.

In the movie *Invictus*, Nelson Mandela spoke about a Victorian poem that gave him strength to carry on when all he wanted to do was to sleep. The poem is called *Invictus* and was written by William Ernest Henley. Henley was always a sickly child growing up and needed to have his left leg amputated below the knee. Frequent illness kept Henley from school but he succeeded in school and went on to Oxford. Henley had troubles with his right foot too and the doctors wanted to amputate that foot as well as it was also diseased. Henley married and had a daughter who died at five years old. Although, Henley had much trauma and pain in his life, he kept moving forward. Mandela stated that during his more than 25 years on Robbins Island Prison this poem gave him strength to get up when all he wanted to do was to lay down.

> Out of the night that covers me (Born into this world)
> Black as the pit from pole to pole (as dark and ugly as it can be)
> I thank whatever god that be (I'm glad that there is a higher power)
> For my unconquerable soul (Larger than life, my soul was created by God)
> In the fell clutch of circumstance (It is what it is)
> I have not winced nor cried aloud (I have not complained)
> Under the bludgeonings of chance (The bad luck of the draw)
> My head is bloody, but unbowed (I'm beat up but not beat)
> Beyond this place of wrath and tears (When I'm dead)
> Looms but the horror of the shade (Death is not the end)
> And yet the menace of the years (As I have gotten older)
> Finds and shall find me unafraid (I'm okay with death)
> It matters not how strait the gate (storms will come)
> How charged with punishments the scroll (persecutions matter not)
> I am the master of my fate (I lived my way)
> I am the captain of my soul (and I am empowered)

The poem explained to me how much power I had on the inside. I not only read the poem but came to interpret it in my own words which are in the parenthesis after each line. I am the master of my fate and I am the captain of my soul. If I maintain a positive countenance, then all will be well. If I continue to look up instead of around, all will be well.

Self-delusion is one of the devil's greatest tools but self-awareness is important if we want to transform our lives. Many times, it only after a tragedy that we start to actually decide to take that painful journey inside to move to a better place. It's only through the self-exploration process that we can understand that we are okay; in fact, we are better than okay, we are great! We are exactly how God intended us to be. We may be bloody but unbowed. I am comfortable with who I am and understand that I can be the whole and healthy person that God wants me to be. Our journey is a pilgrimage and throughout that journey, we will go through sandstorms, droughts and encounter hostile forces. But God, gives us all we need because it's through that hazardous pilgrimage that we learn (if we want) what's important. What ultimately matters is inner peace and joy. Every day a test occurs, we can choose to pass the test or fail the test.

Every day I have a choice, I can be a person who does things pleasing to God, or not. I am now on the road to being whole and healthy because I have chosen to live that way. I have chosen to make my spiritual growth, my first priority. I have chosen to make my God, the most important priority in my life. I decided to get out of my way and let God lead me.

Too many people continue to live broken lives and can only view their world through their defective lenses. Once I surrendered to God, I was given a new God-conscious lens to view the world. My current God-conscious lens is centered on love and positive affirmations for all. It does not matter what you think of me because I just need to do my job. I am no longer carried by the winds of my pride or ego. I just have to follow God's law and put good into the world.

We suffer when we live outside the will of God. The Holy Spirit lives in us but we can't tap into that power when we are negative and living in the flesh. I transformed my life by changing my heart, mind and body. I am now in a right frame of mind and the right frame of heart. I am honest, open and willing to what God wants to teach me now. I continue to make mistakes but willingly accept God's admonishes, direction and His grace. I am mindful each day that I can become better than the day before. I strive with a positively open and loving heart each day to please God.

Apoorve Dubey stated, "*Know yourself, you are unique, priceless and a gift to this world.*"

Chapter 8

Step Six: *Have specific, measurable plans, goals and dreams. Write it down and chart your growth in these three areas: spiritual, mental and physical.*

Why make plans and goals? Plans are important because they give you direction, motivate you and provide a challenge for you. Challenges are helpful for people as they add meaning to our lives which is why people play sports or participate in other endeavors. In making goals, one should think in terms of making short term goals (6-12 months), medium term goals (1-3 years) and long term goals (3-5 years).

Cognitive therapists discuss schemas which are the ways we filter how we see the world. People develop cognitive biases which are the selective ways in which they view and interpret events. People are selective and arbitrary in how they view the events of their lives which is why misunderstandings occur. Further, people tend to generalize events in their memories of the past as well as their current and future viewpoints. Cognitive therapy asserts that most depressed people have learned a highly negative world view or schema through early experiences in childhood or adolescence. Cognitive therapy's goal is to break and then change a pattern of behavior through changes in thinking. One way to help in changing your thinking is to change your actions. Having specific and measurable goals/plans can help you break those old faulty points of views which affect your actions.

It's a fact that many people have such a hard time getting out of their own way. Their old views and beliefs have them in a mental prison. If you say the weather is great, their mind interprets that simple sentence through their faulty or defective world view. These individuals may respond by saying how it supposed to rain tomorrow or in another negative way which gives clues to their irrational or distorted thinking. Some of us suffer from various forms of this but the key to recovering is to know that we all have bias which we can change. Some people have a constant negative world view which leads to a self-fulfilling prophesy about life. Life sucks and then it does suck for that person because everything they do props up and supports that world view. The problem is that people interpret events rather than see them as it actually happens to them. Thoughts, feelings and behaviors tend to be interwoven. You can break the chains that bind you by changing how you think, worship and live.

Many people love to talk about their faulty world view and all it took was a few supporting words from another person to get them to rant about how unfair their boss is or how unfair their spouse is etc. It's only through removing the ego and letting go of the past that you can find your purpose in order to live a life pleasing to God. The Bible says in the Gospel of John that you shall now the truth and the truth shall set you free. In the Holy Qur'an in Surah 41:53, it says, "We will show them Our signs in the world and in themselves, that the truth may be manifested to them. In another section of the Qur'an in Surah 29:69, "Those who strive in Our way, verily We will guide them to the right paths." It's important to know yourself so that you can help yourself to get over the programming of the past. Once you identify your areas of challenge then you can start your new life by making tangible and ambitious plans/goal.

Many people are so afraid to look at themselves that they would rather continue to bump into walls, being led by those base desires and past hurts. It's like a dog which has been abused; he is constantly thinking that the next owner will beat him as well. Have you ever noticed how difficult it is for that dog to trust again? That dog is skittish and afraid of everything even when you try to offer it something good like food. That abused dog has internalized the pain and cannot move beyond it. God has given us a mind and a soul which should allow us to be better than our canine friends. We were created by an amazing God to be able to move beyond the hurts and past programming, so why not make that move today?

Malcolm X said, *"There is no better than adversity. Every defeat, every heartbreak, every loss, contains its own seed, its own lesson on how to improve your performance next time."*

<u>Upon birth, we are given a great commission, find out who we are.</u> We are given great books of wisdom and people who appear in our paths to help us discover what are purposes are. But after we are born, life happens and we are taken off our paths by traumas and pain. But the difficulties help us to become stronger and better people. It's only through these heartaches, that we can find ourselves and learn our true purpose in life. We start to live a life of deeper meaning and significance. Once we find out who we are, the past no longer pains us. I found out who I was through Christ. Once I found out who I was, I created a plan for my life. I developed my plan to build my mind, body and spirit along whole and healthy lines. I advise others to make plans/goals for your life because it helped me greatly to move forward.

Albert Einstein is believed to have stated that the most important decision one can ever make is to decide whether the universe is friendly or hostile. I used to believe that the universe was hostile especially. I did not believe the world to be friendly. But God, made us in a way to be able to change and grow. I started by changing in a very simple way; I decided to view the world in a new friendlier manner. When I did this, a brighter world opened up to me. Einstein also believed in doing "thought experiments". His thought experiments were primarily concerned with the deepest questions about reality and truth. Einstein stated, *"Subtle is the Lord, but malicious He is not."* Some believe that they live in a world aimed against them.

'Know Better' Life Principle: <u>**Your transformation starts inside your mind. Start believing that the universe is friendly.**</u>

In this vein, I came up with a suggested thought experiment or exercise of my own.

'Know Better' Empowerment Exercise: Write on a sheet of paper what type of person you would like to be and then tie your goals to what you wrote. This is an important part of this step, writing down goals to get you there. This will be the start of a different life, if you take it to heart. There was a saying which states that "if we change the way we look at things, then the things we look at, will change."

It's like the thought experiment of Erwin Schrodinger's where he imagined a cat in a sealed box with a poisonous gas released if a particle is emitted. Is the cat alive? We cannot know this until we open the box and observe it thereby fixing the outcome; until then, the cat is neither alive nor dead or both. I liked the above thought because it discusses the possibility of alternate realities. I like to think of a world with alternate realities happening at the same time. I view these alternate realities in my head as events I can draw strength from as there is a reality where I can get it right the first time and other realities I don't but all of them are striving for the same goal -- being whole and healthy -- which gives me strength in my reality.

On my goal sheet, I wrote down the following: "I will put God first. I will live to serve God and help others. I will do what is pleasing to God. I will love as God wants me to love, with my whole heart. I will be whole and healthy and have the same type of relationships in my life. I will help others find their way as I have found my way. I will love everyone. I will show forgiveness to all who have wronged me. I will be kind and charitable to all. I will have honest intentions when dealing with others. I will stay in constant communication with God throughout the day. I will be thankful every day for all I have. I will be a light to others. My life will be an example to others. I believe and will make a great difference in the world. I will pray, love and hope big and boldly every second of the day! In my life, I will expect beauty and kindness in my life every day. I will make sure each day I live that my life is aligned to God's blueprint, the Bible. I will live a life of intentionality by using a strategy based on God's plan for my life. I am joy, love and happy. I am whole." This is how I see myself now and this is how I reach my new whole and healthy goals for life. I decided to reshape and rebuild my life based on healthier principles but it required me having a plan.

This was only a part of my thought experiment as to how I wanted to live my life on a daily basis. I made the above statement a part of my goals and sought to hit my target each day. It's important to change how we see the world but we cannot see a different world still living by old values. Once we changed the way we view the world, the world will change how it views us. My plan focused on God, love, compassion and helping others. I strove to put an ambitious plan on paper for myself.

In my plan, I listed my tools of success and my tools of defeat. In the tools for success section, I wrote, "Prayer, love, hope, optimism, fearlessness, focus, making goals/plans, self-control, forgiveness, charity, purity, generosity, compassion, vision. Tools for failure/defeat: doubt, fear, envy, jealousy, drift, aimlessness, selfishness, lust, greed, hate, anger, holding grudges and the like." I decided to use my tools for success instead of the tools for defeat. The tools of success are provided by God while the tools of defeat are provided by Satan.

There was a quote I love from Reid Hoffman and Ben Casnocha from The Start-up of You which says, *"Take intelligent and bold risks to accomplish something great."*

I believe that my experiences happened so that others could learn. I write with love and gentleness for all of God's creatures. I have compassion for those who are still in the darkness and my prayers are for them as well as my loved ones. I believe in what C.S. Lewis wrote when he said, *"I believe in God as I believe the sun has risen, not because I can see it, but because by way of it, I can see everything else."*

Goals should be SMART: Specific, Measurable, Attainable, Relevant and Time-bound. The goal should be specific. For example, I want to increase my prayer life daily by praying at the top of every hour for one year in order to increase my tangible contact with God. This is specific in that it's at the top of every hour. This goal is measurable and attainable (based on my schedule) as well as relevant and timed bound over one year. SMART goals will transform your life.

I based this goal on something I read in Mark 1:35 which said, "Very early in the morning, while it was still dark, Jesus got up, left the house and went off to a solitary place, where he prayed." I aligned my one spiritual goal to a principle found in the Bible. If prayer was important for Christ then I know it's important for me.

God is unlimited and we were created by a loving, omnipotent God, thus our potential is unlimited but we need to do your part. For example, say if my goal is to relax more to nurture my spirit then I first need to understand the various methods to relax such as deep abdominal breathing, meditation, guided imagery, progressive muscle relaxation, visualizing peaceful scenes etc. From this, I start to set a time each day to start doing a positive daily ritual aimed to help myself. I start with five minutes in the morning and five minutes in the evening but over time I increase my practice using SMART goals.

We are all successful in life. What I mean is that we all aim for certain goals but many times the goals are usually the wrong goals because we are not focusing on the results consciously. For example, if you do not exercise and eat poorly then you are aiming for poor health whether you know it or not. We all know the consequences of that goal; high blood pressure, increased body weight, poor cardiovascular health, etc. So if poor health was your goal then you have hit it in that example, it's the target that you aimed for. Today, I aim for good health and not just a number (my weight) on the scale but when I do the things necessary for good health, I get a healthy number on the scale.

If you want a better life then make a conscious effort to live an abundant life by working step six. Align your new positive inner dialogue to your plan and then move forward in a positive direction with a foundation centered on God and love.

"I find it fascinating that most people plan their vacation with better care that they do their lives. Perhaps that is because escape is easier than change." Jim Rohn

Fitzhugh Dodson stated, *"Without goals, and plans to reach them, you are like a ship that has set sail with no destination."*

Chapter 9

Step Seven: *Smile, it helps bring you joy. Keep joy in your heart despite your external circumstances.*

Why is there a whole step on smiling? Smiling is good for your health and everyone needs to understand how much power this little gesture has over one's life. Researchers have found out that wearing a smile brings about certain benefits like slowing down the heart and reducing stress. The very act of smiling can help you feel better, happier. Upon waking up each morning, I put a smile on my face and immediately feel better even if I am tired or not wanting to get up. Some research has suggested that only a full genuine smile provides benefits while other studies show that even a polite smile may be beneficial. You can influence your mental health by what you do with your face whether you smile a lot or frown a lot. Frowning also has a health effect, but in the opposite direction. So many Americans suffer from anxiety disorders, mood disorders or substance abuse issues. Many of these disorders can be improved by doing our part; exercising, changing our inner dialogue, being positive, establishing a spiritual practice and smiling.

Healthy habits are important in life, and positive daily rituals can help you transform your life. Too many people struggle from day to day barely able to move forward. This is not the way God intended us to live.

"Every time you smile at someone, it is an action of love, a gift to that person, a beautiful thing." Mother Teresa

Socrates stated, "The unexamined life is not worth living." The Bible also mentions this same principle in 1 Corinthians 11:28 where it says, "But let a man examine himself..." Galatians 6:4 states, "But let each one examine his own work..." I decided that I had to look deeply inside myself in order to see where I could improve, get closer to living a life pleasing to God. God wants us to be happy and smiling can help us get there.

Many people are in therapy. I am huge proponent of therapy as it helps people to become self-aware but many times therapy becomes a life-long crutch in lieu of getting better. The only way to get through the pain; is to go through it and travel out the other side. Once we get through it, we are stronger. When we gain insight into our problems, it helps us to heal and move beyond the hurts and traumas of the past but at some point, we have to make the decision to change. Too few people only talk about changing without starting new positive anchor behaviors to move forward. Smiling is one of those new positive anchor behaviors that can help us to pivot. Smiling can improve your health and boost your immune system.

"The best of healers is good cheer." Pindar 500 B.C.

Smiling seems to have so many positive benefits over our health even if science cannot quantify the exact benefits. Smiling opens up so many other intangible doors. People who smile more tend to elicit more positive connections with other people. A smile indicated overall well-being and inner joy. Everyone wants to feel joy.

A study published in the journal Psychological Science in November 2012 found that people who smiled after engaging in stress inducing tasks showed a greater reduction in heart rate than people who maintained a neutral facial expression. The study involved 170 participants and it had each person hold chop sticks in their mouth in three different ways. One way forced the participants to have a neutral expression, another prompted a polite smile and the third resulted in a full smile using the muscles around the mouth and the eyes. The study's results showed a steeper decline in heart rate and a faster physiological stress recovery when they were smiling. This was the result even when they did not know they were smiling. Participants wearing a full smile performed better than the ones with a polite smile.

Doctors explained that we smile because we do not feel threatened. Once that signal is sent to the muscles that you want to smile, the rest of your body and its organs respond as well. Studies have found that the intensity of a person's smile can help predict life satisfaction over time and even longevity.

In the military, they say that one must actively participate in one's own rescue. It's the same with depression. There were so many people walking around with frowns on their faces and they complain all the time, and these behaviors affect our moods. We can help ourselves in fighting depression by smiling even when we do not feel like smiling. It's even more important to smile when you do not feel like smiling because it can move you closer to a better mood. A smile tells your body that everything is okay. So many people walk around with an angry face wondering why they were stressed out and feeling anxious. An expression of anger on your face tells your body that you are not okay and that there is something that you need to be angry about.

In the section on being positive, you have the power to choose your facial expression in spite of your outer circumstances. You can laugh and smile all you want. I try to be a light to others and people often ask me why I am always so happy. I used it as an opportunity to testify for God. "I am happy because God has given me all the conditions for my own happiness right now." Smiling also allows me to put a little bit of goodness into the world.

God has given us all we need to be healthy and the next suggestions can help immensely: Starting an ambitious spiritual practice; thinking differently, being more positive; exercising which helps us physically and mentally; changing that inner and outer dialogue, and smiling. If a person is committed to being good to themselves then there is a solution but it requires effort and being intentional.

I also connect smiling with laughing as well because both help our mood. Laughter has been documented to improve one's health. To help my own mood, I put a smile on my face and then I look for every opportunity to laugh each day. When I can't find an opportunity to laugh, I just laugh anyway. Smiling and laughing can change your life.

I love the beginning of Psalm 126: "When the Lord brought back the captive ones of Zion, We were like those who dream. Then our mouth was filled with laughter and our tongue with joyful shouting; Then they said among the nations. The Lord has done great things for them. The Lord has done great things for us; we are glad." If we make outward expressions of our faith through smiles and laughter then we are showing God how thankful we are. We are putting our faith in action because if we truly cast our cares and worry on God then we should smile because God is taking care of our needs. I believe that when I smile, I show the world that I am trusting in God. Too many people submit to their circumstances. Don't submit to your outer circumstances, but to the Lord who controls circumstances. Carrying your worries or stresses on your face will only magnify your worries.

In the Buddhist's Book the Dhammapada, it says, "*All that we are is the result of what we have thought: all that we are is founded on our thoughts and formed of our thoughts.*" A smile is a physical 'thought of goodness' put into action. There is a process for self-transformation and it starts with a smile. In this process of self-transformation, it's critical to strengthen our inner nature in order to master the outer self. But at the same time, there are things we can do on the outside which helps the inner person such as working out, smiling, and eating in a healthy manner.

I have mentioned that people settle for too less out of life. They limit themselves and their dreams to such a degree; they forget who they were created to be. God created us to be whole and healthy living a life of purpose and meaning. We can move toward perfection. The quest for human perfection is expressed in many of the classic works of Eastern tradition and in the works of the Judeo/Christian and Islamic traditions. The New Testament refers to "just men made perfect."

We have the power inside of us where we could reach a higher level of spiritual attainment but we need to do things differently. We all have emotional wounds, hurts and disappointments that we are trying to deal with. Stop trying to deal with it, and just deal do it now. When you are stressed out, smile. When you are feeling sad, smile. Smiling is free therapy. Now, I attempt each day maintain a balanced mood so I use a smile to maintain good overall health. Give the gift of a smile to someone today!

Smiling creates positive energy and a positive vibration. There are people who always have low energy and continue to perpetuate that low energy with their negative words and thoughts. We have the power to be what God intended us to be. Smiling can open up waves of positive energy and blessings into your life.Start your day with a smile no matter how you feel, and you will immediately feel better.

"Don't cry because it's over. Smile because it happened." Dr. Seuss

I started my day with a positive ritual of smiling, then praying followed by reading the Bible. We can consciously decide how are day will go by just starting with a smile and then maintaining it throughout the day. Many of us have internalized negative daily rituals which lead to a life of negativity. I evaluated all of my thoughts and actions in order to eliminate those which were negative while at the same time starting new positive daily rituals. If I only had a few minutes then I would split my routine up so that I could start my day off with a positive daily ritual regardless what was going on around me.

In the world, so many people are negatively affected by those around them. I refused to be affected by the circumstances around me. I would confound some around me who asked me how I could smile while there were bad things are happening in the world. I advised those who asked me that question that I was only responsible for doing my job every day. My job consists of putting God first; loving all, helping all, forgiving all, using the tools God gave me in a productive fashion so as to honor God, and being a light for those who are still in the darkness. Doing my job is not dependent on anyone else doing their job because my boss is God and I have to answer to him. I smile because I have embraced my new job with passion and diligence.

To create a positive mental image of yourself, start with a smile each day and throughout the day. Gospel great Kirk Franklin has a song called "I smile". I love this song and play it often because it's so beautiful. The song says, "I smile even though I hurt, see I smile. I know God is working, so I smile. Even though I've been here a while I smile... I smile it's so hard to look up when you've been down. Sho would hate to see you give up now, you look so much better when you smile. So smile.... Smile for me. Can you just smile for me. You look so much better when you smile." These are only a few of the lyrics of this song but it's so true. We honor God when we smile because we tell the world that we are trusting God. Kirk Franklin says that he wants us to have joy because no one can take that away from us. It's the same with your smile; no one can take your smile away unless you let them.

It's hard to be depressed when you are smiling. It's hard to be thankful for everything God gives us when we are frowning. It's easy to praise God with a smile but not so much when you are angry. Every morning I set up my lemonade stand so that anything that comes my way I will be prepared to accept it and make lemonade out of those lemons.

I made a decision to open my heart and my spiritual ears in order to hear all that God was trying to tell me. We live in a world of negative behaviors each day, but we have a choice. We are empowered. I smile all throughout the day because God has given us the power to overcome anything, and you can too. I want the world to know that I trust in God with all my heart, soul and mind.

In sum, smiling lowers our heart rate, reduces stress, improves mood, produces empathy and trust, makes us look younger and more attractive, and boost our immune system. Smiling is free and contagious. If you see someone without a smile today, give them yours.

I smile because I know that everything will be okay. It will be okay for you too, just smile!

Mother Teresa stated that, *"We shall never know all the good a simple smile can do."*

"Let my soul smile through my heart and my heart smile through my eyes, that I may scatter rich smiles   in   sad   hearts."   Paramahansa Yogananda

Chapter 10

Step Eight: *Help others, volunteer. Sow seeds of love. Be a blessing to others daily. Be a light to others.*

I will use Jesus' words to start this section:

"But I say to you who hear, Love your enemies, do good to those who hate you. Bless those who curse you, and pray for those who spitefully use you. To him who strikes you on one cheek, offer the other also. And from him who takes your cloak, do not withhold your tunic either. Give to everyone who asks of you. And him who takes away your goods do not ask them back. And just as you want men to do to you, you also do to them likewise. But if you love those who love you, what credit is that to you? For even sinners love those who love them. And if you do good to those who do good to you, what credit is that to you. For even sinners do the same. And if you lend to those whom you hope to receive back, what credit is that to you? For even sinners lend to sinners to receive as much back. But love your enemies, do good, and lend, hoping for nothing in return; and your reward will be great, and you will be the sons of the Most High (Luke 6:27-35)."

Many people read this section and look for loopholes but I decided to do something different, obey. I exchanged my old programming for new programming. I surrendered and got a different result out of life. Imagine how much better the world would be if we all strived to live by the above words.

All of these steps feed into one another. The last step discussed how smiling can transform your life. I wanted to provide another quote to get this section started.

"The face is the mirror of the mind, eyes without speaking confess the secrets of the heart." Saint Jerome.

One smile can help others as it can show others that we care about them. Sometimes all it takes to help others is just an encouraging word or a smile. Many people often try to commiserate with other person by joining in when that person is complaining about a situation but that is feeding the wrong side of the equation. Feed the positive by focusing on God's blessing, not the devil's curses. In the workplace, often one person starts complaining and then another, before long everyone is upset and the energy becomes negative. There are times when we can insert ourselves into a situation and provide a positive word, not feeding the negative but the positive and the whole dynamic can change. We have that power as well. Changing the inner and outer dialogue (step 2), being positive (step 5) and smiling (step 7) all work towards in helping others, being that light in the world that we want to see. Step one discussed being good and gentle with yourself which will start the transformation process. Once that step has begun and you are truly good to yourself then you can start being good to others by sowing seeds of love.

The prayer of St. Francis of Assisi provided me with great guidance with this step in terms of how to live.

> *Lord, make me an instrument of your peace:*
> *where there is hatred, let me bring love;*
> *where there is wrong, let me bring the spirit of forgiveness;*
> *where there is discord, let me bring harmony;*
> *where there is error, let me bring truth;*
> *where there is doubt, let me show faith;*
> *where there is despair, let me sow hope;*
> *where there is darkness, let me sow light;*
> *where there is sadness, let me sow joy;*
> *O divine Master,*
> *grant that I may not so much seek to be comforted as to comfort others,*
> *instead of being understood, let me understand,*
> *instead of being loved, as to love,*
> *For it is in giving that we receive,*
> *it is in pardoning that we are pardoned.*
> *It is in dying that we are born to eternal life. Amen.*

In providing service to others, we help ourselves. Mother Teresa spent her whole life showing compassion and loving in the service of God. Mother Teresa said that, "*we have been created for greater things, to love and be loved.*" She had an aphorism she used in expressing her views:

"*The fruit of silence is prayer; the fruit of prayer is faith; the fruit of faith is love; the fruit of love is service and the fruit of service is peace.*"

Mother Teresa believed that wholehearted service given to Christ to help others was the ultimate way to show love for God. We all need to seek God wholeheartedly and seek to find Him every day. I loved Mother Teresa's phrase that says, "*...true holiness consists in doing God's will with a smile.*" We all know that God loves a cheerful giver.

'Know Better' Empowerment Exercise: Wherever you are having a problem or a challenge in your life whether at home, in the office, at church or at school, plan to sow a seed of love this week. Do something that you have never done before such as bring donuts to the office or pay your greatest enemy a compliment or compliment someone you never have before. Sow a seed of love and it will come back to you. Each day, try to be a blessing to someone each day. Do at least one thing to bless another person. It will make you feel good, to help others. I believe that if we do good deeds without the expectation of receiving a benefit, we are being the hands and feet of Christ.

We all harbor resentments and bitterness in our hearts but this step will help us to clean our hearts. This step helped me to move beyond the hurts of the past. This step is about doing our job and not worrying about what others may think or do to us. My job is to sow seeds of love regardless of what others do. My job is to be a light in the world, not to add to the darkness. I surrendered and understand that it only matters what God thinks of me. If I do my job for God, then I am doing my Father's work. Too many people get stuck in their own drama or other people's drama. God does not like drama as evidenced in His word.

My job is not dependent on you doing your job. This was how I liberated myself by thinking in a new way. The old me would worry about whether you liked me or respected me but I don't care what you think of me now because I don't need your approval, only God's approval. You don't need my approval either, only God's approval. This new way of thinking was part of my spiritual awakening. Too few people focus on doing things in a way that would make God happy but instead worry about what would make another defective human happy. I had it backwards and many others have it backwards as well.

You have to see yourself as whole and healthy, and plan accordingly so that you must make that goal a habit in your daily life. In that vein, being selfless allows us to get out of our own way. If we help others and volunteer, then we are doing something that helps us connect with God.

In the AA 12 step program, it states that one can only keep what one has (sobriety) by giving it away and helping others. I never understood this principle previously until I sought out God by reading His book. I stopped looking for someone to save me, but started relying on God. Humans disappoint but God never disappoints. When I started focusing on just doing my job-- being a light for others, the transformation process started inside me.

Transformation can only occur on the inside. One can't heal the wounds or traumas from the past looking outside of oneself. It takes hard work and occurs on the inside. Once you begin that difficult work on the inside, you will see that you are okay and can get better. Be the change you want to see in the world. It's possible, if you have a larger vision.

As the prayer of St. Francis says, seek to help others. If you are depressed, help others. Giving without an expectation of receiving anything in return will provide its own benefits. If you are depressed and are already helping others, then help more people and sow more seeds of love. It's easy to help people who we like, but God wants us to help all people. There are so many intangible benefits from helping those who you may not like or agree with or even have a grudge against. Doing a little favor for someone can earn you a new friend. Jesus wants us to help others.

A willing and open heart defines how we sow our seeds. If we eventually do something for someone but do it without love, then we have not done it in the manner God intended us to do it in. This step is about love because we are commissioned to be the hands and feet of Christ. If we love then we want to help others find what we have found. If we don't have love then we should work hard to develop that quality.

I did not ever see helping others as something I needed to do in the past. I always did things for an expected reward, quid pro quo (something for something). Now, after reading the bible and creating the principles of my 20 steps, I started to feel differently about myself. Helping others, helps us and assists us in feeling better about ourselves.

Psychologists say that if we want to change a habit then we will need to replace it out for another habit. I changed my behavior after reading about love in the Bible. I didn't at first understand why it was important to help others but once I started then I realized why. If Jesus took time to help others, then so should we. I changed my negative behavior for more positive behavior. I added into my behavior the various practices of meditation, prayer, worship and helping others to my old habits. Once I replaced my old habits with new habits, the new habits became more natural and easier to do.

As I started practicing my steps, it became easier to sow more seeds. There was a multiplicative effect that allowed me to become a better person. Every day I wake up, I look for opportunities to help others. I would tell those who I help to pay it forward, to help someone else so that my gift would have a ripple effect.

Step 8 can change the world if we all start to replace our existing behaviors with habits that sow seeds of love. These habits will put positive energy in the world and could help someone who may be at the end of their rope and desperate. An act of kindness shows others that they are not alone. Another way of sowing seeds of love is to tell others that we love them. This little act of kindness can make a difference to others.

So many people try to find happiness in things but it's the inner person which will transform us. Jesus said, "Take heed and beware of covetousness for one's life does not consist in the abundance of the things he possesses." God sowed the greatest seed of love when he gave up His son for us (John 3:16). It is our reasonable duty to try and sow our own seeds.

Separately but related, everyone has a mission to fulfill in life. Colossians 4:17 states, "...Take heed to the ministry which you have received in the Lord, that you may fulfill it." The word "ministry' can be exchanged with the phrase "serving God". We were created by God for a purpose. Everything that God has created has a purpose. We matter to God and it's our job to serve Him and to bring glory to His name. Our purpose or ministry is connected to why God created us. When we accept Christ into our hearts, then it's time to go to work because we are given a second chance. "All things work together for good to those who love God, to those who are called according to His purpose (Romans 8:28)." We are all called to bring others to Christ. We are all meant to be ministers of Christ. Peter tells us that we were chosen by God "to do His work and speak out for Him, to tell others of the night and day difference He made for you (1

Peter 2:9)." Jesus stated in Mathew 28:18-20, "...All Authority has been given to Me in heaven and earth. 'Go therefore and make disciples of all nations, baptizing them in the name of the Father, and of the Son and of the Holy Spirit, teaching them to observe all things that I have commanded you; and lo, I am with you always, even to the end of this age.' Amen." This is called the great commission and it was given by Jesus to His disciples but it's also His commission to us. Living with love and serving with love, will ignite the fire within!

In 2 Corinthians 9:6, we learn that, "...He who sows sparingly will also reap sparingly, and he who sows bountifully will also reap bountifully." Lights produce more light.

"Only a life lived in the service of others is worth living." Albert Einstein

Lynne Namka stated, *"Love in action is service to the world."*

One of my favorite quotes about helping others is by Mahatma Gandhi, *"The best way to find yourself is to lose yourself in the service of others."*

Chapter 11

Step Nine: *Understand who you are, what you are and how much power you have inside through how God sees you. God is within us and has given us the power to be whatever we want to be.*

"The most common way people give up their power is by thinking they don't have any." Alice Walker

We have within us, power to do amazing and miraculous things. "Do you not know that your body is the temple of the Holy Spirit who is in you, whom you have from God, and you are not your own? For you were brought at a price, therefore glorify God in your body and in your spirit, which are God's (1 Corinthians 6:19-20)." We can attain a higher state but we must honor God with our gifts. I have composed a list of scriptures from the Bible at the end of this work to help all of us keep God first place in our hearts. Living by the verses of the Bible will open up a new world to us.

"The Spirit God gave us does not make us timid, but gives us power, love and self-discipline (2 Timothy 1:7)." I didn't understand who I was before I was saved nor the consequences of all of my actions even the good ones. Today, my actions are focused on what is good for me as a whole and healthy person who lives for God. I have joy in my heart finally after so many years, and the world did not give it to me and the world cannot take it away from me. I have joy because of my God.

'Know Better' Life Principle: **The world cannot give you joy, only God can bring real inner peace. Once you start on this journey to strengthen your inner person, the world cannot take away your joy.**

2 Corinthians 5:17 is a powerful part of this step. "Therefore, if anyone is in Christ, he is a new creation; old things have passed away; behold, all things have become new." Memorize, believe and take this verse to heart. I can't be a new creation if I do the same old things. We have much power within us but we can only connect with it until we understand who we are.

Psalm 37:4 says, "Delight yourself in the Lord, and He shall give you the desires of your heart." I believe that one can only delight oneself in the Lord by following his commandments and statutes. When we follow God's way, we are empowered.

Isaiah 40:31 provides additional insight, "But those who wait on the Lord shall renew their strength; they shall mount up with wings like eagles, they shall run and not be weary. They shall run and not faint." Once I started living for God, I begin to have more energy than I ever had before. Just the act of meditating and thinking about God during the day empowered me.

God explains to us how we should live when He said, "Fear not, for I am with you; Be not dismayed, for I am your God. I will strengthen you, Yes, I will help you, I will uphold you with my righteous right hand (Isaiah 41:10)." Three verses later, it's repeated, "For I, the Lord your God, will hold your right hand, Saying to you, 'Fear not, I will help you' (Isaiah 41:13)." So many people live with fear and dread each day. I used to live this way when I lived in the flesh and had a weak foundation in Godly principles but God wants us to live an elevated life of abundance and plenty.

God has a plan for each of us. Jeremiah 29:11-14 explains it clearly, "I alone knows the plans I have for you, plans to bring you prosperity and not disaster, plans to bring about your future you hoped for. Then you will call upon me and go and pray to Me, and I will answer you. And you will seek Me and find Me, (the burden is on us) when you search for Me with all of your heart (not a part of your heart but all of your heart). I will be found by you (a promise), says the Lord, and I will bring you back from your captivity (the captivity of our sins and our defective thinking). The words in the parenthesis are mine.

God has given us all we need. We are God's greatest creation and we have amazing power within us. No one can judge you or make you feel less than you are, unless you let them. You have the power to not believe what other defective humans say about you and the power to believe what the Almighty Lord of the Worlds, the great I AM WHO I AM, says about you!

Psalm 118:24-25 says "This is the day the Lord has made, we will rejoice and be glad in it. Save now, I pray, send now prosperity." So many people view the world through their defective worldly lenses instead of how God sees them. Believe what God says about you and what is possible through faith in Him.

'Know Better' Life Principle: **You will always be as strong as you think you are. No one can hurt you with words unless you give them power to. You are empowered!**

Too many people allow the hurts from the past to color their future. This is why I love Philippians 3:12-14 written by the Apostle Paul from a Roman prison. Paul stated, "Not that I have already attained, or am already perfected; but I press on, that I may lay hold of that for which Christ Jesus has also laid hold of me. Brother, I do not count myself to have apprehended; but one thing I do, forgetting those things which are behind and reaching forward to those things which are ahead. I press toward the goal for the prize of the upward cal of God in Christ Jesus." We must move beyond the pains of the past to move into the blessing that God has in store for us.

Paul did not speak about how bad things were, to complain but to explain how it strengthened him. Paul was in prison and stated in Philippians 4:11 that, "I have learned in whatever state I am, to be content." Paul learned to be content and we can learn as well. Two verses later Paul stated how he could do all things through Christ who strengthened him (Philippians 4:13). When Paul mentioned his trials, he explained that it was for the glory of God and how those problems benefited him. According to his writings, Paul did not see himself as a victim and neither should you. You will stop being a victim once you stop thinking like a victim.

Ralph Waldo Emerson wrote, *"Be not slave of your own past. Plunge into the sublime seas, dive deep, and swim far, so you shall come back with self-respect, with new power, with an advanced experience, that shall explain and overlook the old."*

Each of us has to realize at some point that there are many different paths. One path says that we should believe what others think about us. A second path tells us to go after external objects to satisfy our basic urges. A third path says that I know there is more out here than what I can see but I cannot obtain it. A fourth path advises us that there is a solution to our plight but we veer off the path. The last path is one that is so clear that when we find it, we are surprised that it took us this long to find it- this path is of God and is love.

'Know Better' Life Question: There is no path to love, love is the path. Which path are you on?

'Know Better' Empowerment Exercise: Tell yourself, "I'm believing God. God is who He says He is. God can do what He says He can do. I am who God says I am. I can do all things through Christ. God's word is alive and active in me!" Tell yourself this statement every morning and/or throughout the day when feeling in the dumps or with low energy.

Don't be oblivious to a world of infinite possibilities. The universe is not stacked against you. God is for you! In James 4:8, we learn that if we draw near to God then God will draw near to us. There is a better way but pride and stubbornness continues to hinder us at times. These negative emotions are important ones for Satan because it moves us in a direction away from God.

I transformed my thinking by changing how I viewed the world and my Maker. I changed how I looked at all my tribulations; because now I see them as learning experiences. God sent His son, Jesus Christ, to die for my sins, and your sins. I came to internalize that I was special, not because of what I do but because God thought so much of me that he sent His only son to die for me. My value was no longer in what I owned or what I wore or what others thought of me; my value is being a son of the Most High God and this can never change. I have the power and you have the power! The power was given to us by God and can be only taken away by God.

We are God's masterpiece and His most prized possession but unfortunately too few people view themselves this way. Don't forget how to be thankful and to enjoy life's little blessings. There are so many people walking around with a beaten down mentality. As such, these people ridicule and belittle others throughout the day. Many still walk around each day with frowns or angry looks on their faces. Recognize your true worth through Christ as a way to fight the sadness, anger and negativity of the world.

My primary goal now is to introduce people to God and Christ Jesus but also to let those who had fallen down know that there is a better way. I want everyone to understand that they have the power. Although I used to define myself by the illusions in my lives, I now know who I am in Christ Jesus. You can define yourself through Christ too. Nothing on the outside that we buy is going to repair the damage on the inside. There is a different way. You can move beyond the disappointment and hurts of the past.

Once I opened my eyes and was born again, I was struck by the absurdity of how I lived. I realized I was like a mouse in a maze looking for that cheese. Zombie-land is real and many people operate on base instincts like a zombie going from one impulse to another. To get off the gerbil wheel of life, we must first understand who we are. Sometimes, falling down is the best thing to ever happen to us because it allows us to start to look at life differently (if we see the lesson that God is trying to show us). We were created to live a life of wonder, not of desperation.

Some of us have forgotten who we are and some of us never knew who we were. In this world of tabloid media, reality shows feature dysfunction, defective and hurting people. It seems in today's society that normal is considered abnormal and the abnormal is considered normal. This step is about understanding who we are. Some people may not have a clue who they are or what it states in 1 John 4:4 which says "we are of God." We dishonor ourselves and the Spirit in us when we speak or live negatively or in an evil manner.

As a child we have to master new things to grow. It's the same now in that we need to master new things. In 2 Timothy 1:6, the Apostle Paul reminds Timothy to rekindle the gift of God that was in him. Although Timothy was loyal and dependable, he apparently struggled with being timid, just as we do sometimes. Paul explained that God's power was at work in him.

The power within us is connected to the Holy Spirit which dwells in us. The ability to transform ourselves in within us but we need to take a different path in this perverse generation. Romans 12:2 states, "And do be conformed to this world but be transformed by the renewing of your mind, that you may prove what is good and acceptable and perfect will of God." I renewed my mind once I was able to "be still and know that I am God (Psalm 46:10)."

In literature, a tragic flaw is a character trait that causes a downfall of a story's hero. I had a lot of tragic flaws just like many people out here. I have had a chance to look inside and reconfigure those character traits along a higher spiritual framework. I finally came to realize that I was fighting the wrong battles. "Thus says the Lord to you: Do not be afraid nor dismayed because of this great multitude, for the battle is not yours, but God's (2 Chronicles 20:15)."

"The most beautiful people we have known are those who have known defeat, suffering, struggle, loss and have found their way out of the depths. These people have an appreciation, sensibility and understanding of life that fills them with compassion, gentleness and a deep loving concern. Beautiful people do not just happen." Elisabeth Kuber-Ross.

Henry Ford said, "*There isn't a person anywhere who isn't capable of doing more than he thinks he can.*"

"*Just because you don't have the answer, doesn't mean there isn't an answer. Remember that God has the answer!*" Philip Allan Turner

Chapter 12

Step 10: *Love God!!! Love everyone especially yourself. Let your love show through your actions. Do everything with love, radical love.*

There is no path to love, love is the path.

In the Webster's Third New International Unabridged Dictionary, it says that **love** is that attraction, desire or affection felt for a person who arouses delight or admiration or elicits tenderness, sympathetic interest, or benevolence, devoted affection. A man's adoration of God in gratitude and devotion. To cherish or foster with divine love and mercy. For example, "I have loved you with an everlasting love," as stated in Jeremiah 31:3. To feel reverent adoration for God as detailed in Exodus 20:6 which says, "...but showing steadfast love to thousands of those who love me and keep my commandments."

The most important concept in being a Christian, is love. There is a song which say, "They will know we are Christians by our love." The love Jesus spoke of was a radical type of love, it was radical for that time and is still considered radical now.

'Know Better' Life Principle: **Love is the very nature of God. God is love and we are of God.**

I never thought about loving God before I was born again. I never knew how much God loved me and never knew that His love for me was unconditional and steadfast, unlike the dysfunctional human love we have become accustomed to. Romans 8:38-39 stated, "I am persuaded that neither death nor life, not angels nor principalities nor powers, nor things present nor things to come, nor height nor depth, nor any other created things, shall be able to separate is from the love of God which is in Christ Jesus our Lord."

For me to really love myself in a whole and healthy manner, I had to understand what I meant to God and how much he loved me. Once I realized how God felt about me, I was able to start the process of loving myself because if God believed I was worthy to love then I should believe the same as well. I was worthy of love, regardless of my past, thus I could love myself and start to truly love others.

In Ephesians 5:1-2, Paul tells us to "Therefore be imitators of God as dear children, and walk in love, as Christ also has loved us and given Himself for us, an offering and a sacrifice to God for a sweet-smelling aroma." Walking in love is the challenge for all of us.

First and foremost, we need live by the principle of love; which means that we strive to love with our whole heart. To love, we must be able to listen deeply. When we read scripture, we should look for and listen for that small still voice of God. Further, we can show love to others by listening deeply. To love, we should seek to know deeply about others. This is how I learned how much God loves me, by reading His word.

Mother Teresa stated that love was faith in action. She said, *"Our work, to be faithful and to be all for God, and beautiful, has been built on faith -- faith in Christ..."* She expounded, *"On these words of His, all our work is based...Faith to be true has to be a giving love. Love and faith go together. They complete each other."*

If we are faithful to God then we would not fear nor would we hate. "There is no fear in love, but full-grown love turns fear out of doors and expels every trace of terror! For fear brings with it thoughts of punishment, and so he is afraid has not reached the full maturity of love (1 John 4:18)."

I did not understand what love was about or what I had to do to love someone else. I never knew how to love in a whole and healthy manner until I fell in love with God. Following a true Christian life became my new goal. If I could love all those who crossed my path whether they were good to me or not then I could love myself. Before knowing God through His word, I never said, "God, I love you." Now, I say it all day long.

In the Bible, God is described in many ways but I wanted to focus on a few points. God describes himself as, "I am that I am (Ex 3:14)." "God is love (1 John 4:8, 4:16)." "God is a loving Father (Matthew 6:25-32)." "God is in your heart (Romans 10:8)." "God is joy, God is light (John 8:12)." "God is truth (John 14:6)." "God so loved the world that He gave His only begotten Son that who believes shall have everlasting life (John 3:16)." Loving God is about trusting God. Love fulfills the law; and resists vengeance, cruelty, and revenge.

Oliver Wendell Holmes stated, *"Love is the master key that opens the gates of happiness."*

For years, I knew that something was missing in my life because I was incredibly unhappy. I had a good job but I was so unhappy and did not know what was wrong with me personally. I worked hard hoping for the approval of my colleagues in an attempt to feel better about myself. I was hoping if I did well then I would feel better, happier. I didn't even know how important love was to the equation. I did not know how my past conditioning figured into my current state.

I had to ask myself, "Can I love and be loved in a healthy way?" I said no at first but once I changed my thinking and how I viewed the world--it became so clear. The love was inside of me all the time. Now that I have learned how to love God, life has become easier. Since I could love God and myself, I am now prepared to love others with my whole heart.

I realized after I completed my own self-inventory that I needed to learn how to love and be loved in a whole and healthy manner. The devil does not want us to love God nor love others. The devil wants us to blame God for our problems. It's through our problems and tribulations that we become better; more complete humans. Sometimes, we need heartache to understand how to love more fully. We need the low times to be fully able to appreciate the great beauty in life.

Whatever you do in your life, do it with love. There was a song which said that a person was looking for love in all the wrong places. One can substitute the word 'God' in that sentence because many of us are looking for God in all the wrong places too. We need to learn how to look at others through our heart.

Sophocles said, "One word frees us of all the weight and pain of life. That word is love." If you are sick or sad or depressed, you can heal yourself by learning how to love.

The Apostle Paul tells us what love is and isn't in 1 Corinthians 13, the chapter on love. 1 Corinthians 13 is called the chapter of love because it defines love through a Godly lens. "Though I speak with the tongues of men and of angels but have not love, I have become a sounding brass or a clanging cymbal. And though I have the gift of prophecy, and understand all mysteries and all knowledge, and through I have all faith, so that I could remove mountains, but have not love, I am nothing. And though I bestow all my goods to feed the poor, and though I give my body to be burned, but have not love, it profits me nothing. Love suffers long and is kind; love does not envy, love does not parade itself, is not puffed up; does not behave rudely, does not seek its own, is not provoked, thinks no evil; does not rejoice in iniquity, but rejoices in truth; bears all things, believes all things, hopes all things. Love never fails... And now abide in faith, hope, love, these three; but the greatest of these is love."

Paul also explains in Romans 12:9-10 when he writes, "Let love be without hypocrisy. Abhor what is evil. Cling to what is good. Be kindly affectionate to one another with brotherly love, in honor giving preference to one another." Romans 13:10 says, "Love does no harm to a neighbor; therefore love is the fulfillment of the law.

1 John 4:7-8 states it clearly as well, "Beloved, let us love one another, for love is of God; and everyone who loves is born of God and knows God. He who does not love does not know God, for God is love." Later in John 4:18-19, "There is no fear in love; but perfect love casts out fear, because fear involved torment. But he who fears has not been made perfect. We love Him because He first loved us." Love dispels fear. Having faith is about trusting and loving God. Faith and fear are opposites and can't exist in the same space.

There are many who would read these words and instead of looking for ways to understand how to integrate the principles of love into their life; they would seek to question and look for holes in how these concepts are not applicable to them. Those individuals are not looking to learn how to love with their whole heart but rather seeking to justify loving in their same defective manner. I was socialized to love in a defective way and had to learn how to retrain myself to love through a Godly lens.

I became whole, healthy and balanced by focusing on finding the love inside and then using that love; to love God, myself, and others helping me to recover. Living in the light allows me to stay centered on love. "For you were once darkness, but now you are light in the Lord. Walk as children of light (Ephesians 5:8)."

In Galatians 5:22, it discusses the fruits of the spirit; and the first fruit of the spirit is love. Love is so important in living a God-centered life. Love is powerful and can heal the wounds of the past if we love with our whole heart. To love with our whole heart, we must eradicate any unforgiveness and hatred for others. Our hearts should be pure in order to love fully and completely.

No one knows how much love the human heart can hold because there is no limit to the amount of love inside of you. I repeat this fact because it's important for us to remember this truth. The Bible says in Ecclesiastes 3:11, "God has put eternity in the human heart." I love this verse because it gives me hope.

I started loving everyone and that started the healing process. I begin by praying for anyone who has ever wronged me and then started asking God to bring them closer to God as He had brought me closer to Him. I started asking God to help everyone in my life. Loving big and boldly will give you the strength to move beyond any old hurts.

"Love is the most powerful and still most unknown energy in the world." Pierre Teihard de Chardin.

Love is powerful in ways that we can't even fathom. I believe love's power is based on the fact that its powerful, positive energy expands out into the universe with our name on it. With that energy being channeled outward, an equal amount of positive energy will be sent back to you in return. Love is a life force which produces its own curative energies. Love can empower and strengthen any hurts, disappointments, and traumas.

Saint Teresa of Avila stated that, *"Love draws forth love."*

Love connects us with the energy in the universe; that energy is the abundant energy of God. When we hold grudges or actually hate others, it interrupts the power of love. If we love everyone then a newfound sense of positive energy will begin to channel the energies of the universe. The goal should be to open up our hearts to the universe. We do not have to move our enemies in our houses but we do have to forgive them and move beyond the old hurts by loving them. If we begin to love with our whole heart, then our lives will change exponentially.

Loving others is like sowing positive energy or seeds in the world. "In the morning sow your seed, and in the evening do not withhold your hand; for you do not know which will prosper (Ecclesiastes 11:6)."

Depression is connected to not loving. There are many people who just need to open their hearts to love.

"When God's divine love rises as a wave, it washes away the sins of a whole life in a moment, for law has no power to stand before love; the stream of life sweeps it away." Hazrat Inayat Khan.

Love should be pure and simple without complicated ulterior motives. Love should be consistent. Love should be done deeply and with a passion. The Bible says that we should love God with all of our heart, mind, soul, and strength. We should love others in a healthy manner with the same passion not just those who love us in return but everyone. For love to be used as a force of good, our core needs to change so that love becomes our default. Someone hurts us, we show them love. Jesus said do not repay evil with evil but good. We need to change our core so that it's full of love for everyone.

To that end, if you are harboring any grudges or biases against anyone, you should strive to love them even more. Work on loving them despite what they may have done to you. It will change your life for the better. Trust God to know what is good for you; loving others is good for you on every level.

God created us. God is love thus our inner nature is one of love but through past conditioning, we have forgotten. We have been taken off the path of love and so we need to relearn how to love.

Once our heart thaws and opens up, we can begin to allow the love to flow through us which builds a sense of inner joy and contentment within our soul. How do we learn to love in a new God-conscious ways? I will use some more Biblical scriptures to provide some additional thoughts below. "Walk in love... (Ephesians 5:2)." What does this mean? Have you ever thought about your daily walk, whether it's in love. It's the little details that show we have love inside.

"Now may the Lord direct your hearts into the love of God and into the patience of Christ (2 Thessalonians 3:5)." The definition of love in this fallen world is so dysfunctional. Almost everything that we see on TV or hear today shows dysfunctional types of love. We have to retrain ourselves in how to love and the perfect model of real love is described by God in the Bible.

We should strive to love with our whole heart in a healthy and Godly way. Many people keep little pockets of negativity in their hearts but we must learn to open those small dark areas in the back of our hearts to God and His love. The Bible offers God inspired examples of how to retrain ourselves in order to love in the right ways.

'Know Better' Life Question: How would you define love?

I will attempt to define love. Love is steadfast. Love is not an emotion; it's a command from God. Love is not a feeling, because feelings come and go. Too often we let our feelings get in the way of our progress. Love is a perfect belief, ordered by God. Love is giving and forgiving. Love is freely given without any expectation of return. Compassion is the emotion we feel when love moves through our hearts. Love does not do right for the wrong reasons. Love is about helping others. Love is "of God" and of the light. Love has nothing to do with attraction because love transcends attraction. God loves us completely and commands us to love others in the same way, not just those who are loveable. Love doesn't keep a record of wrongs. Love doesn't care about the past, because love is pure. Love is an action. Love requires effort, and that effort puts us closer to God. Love is a commandment, not a choice if a person wants to be a follower of Christ. We must strive to learn how to love, using the template from God's word as the framework. Unpack and discard all those old dysfunctional notions of love today.

We learn in Colossians 3:2 that we should, "Set your minds on things above, not on things on the earth." Our love must come from God, and then we should spread it to others.

Jesus commands us "to love God with all our heart, soul, and mind. And then our neighbor as ourselves." What is left unsaid but which is vitally important is that we love ourselves first. We need to love ourselves in a healthy way so that we can give love to others. So many people do not love themselves through and through, they live with guilt, condemnation, shame, and other negative feelings from the past. Christ died on the cross so that we could have salvation and be redeemed through His blood. Christ has forgiven us, forgive yourself, and move on. When we allow those negative emotions or beliefs about ourselves to inhabit our heart, we limit the blessings in our lives.

A person without real love inside their heart cannot give real love to others. We can't give others what we don't have. This is why it's so important to retrain ourselves to love as God has instructed us to love.

Colossians 3:12-17 describes the character of the new person. We should allow love to change us, make us new. The below section from Colossians gives a perfect framework of love.

"Therefore, as the elect of God, holy and beloved, put on tender mercies, kindness, humility, meekness, longsuffering; bearing with one another, and forgiving one another, if anyone has a complaint against another; even as Christ forgave you, so you must do, but above all these things put on love, which is the bond of affection. And let the peace of God rule your hearts, which is the bond of perfection. Let the word of Christ dwell in you richly in all wisdom, teaching and admonishing one another in psalms and hymns and spiritual songs, singing with grace in your hearts to the Lord. And whatever you do in word or deed, do all in the name of the Lord Jesus, giving thanks to God the Father through Him."

Love allowed to deeply move inside our heart allows inner peace to reign in that same place. We need to find ourselves through God and ask Him, "What is Your will for my life?" God is love and His essence of perfect love is already inside our heart, spirit, and soul.

'Know Better' Empowerment Exercise: Tell yourself each morning, "I will see myself as God sees me, a being of light and love!

Plato stated, "He whom love touches, not walks in darkness." Anyone can benefit from coming to a deeper understanding of a radical or revolutionary type of love. We are commanded to love others as God loves us. If our hearts are corrupted with grudges, hate, and other un-Godlike emotions/feelings, we are not following God's commandment about love, and this impedes our blessings. This is why I say that I want to be a radical person who loves without limits, even those who despise or hate me. I strive to love everyone, even the unlovable ones because there were times in my life when I was unlovable, and God still loved me.

I must repeat what the Apostle Paul wrote in 1 Corinthians 13:13, "And now these three remains: faith, hope and love. But the greatest is love."

Wake up every morning and ask God, "Lord, help to show radical love to all of your children. Let your radical love shine through me, to others." Stand firm and live radically in love every day; love as God loves, forgive as God forgives and hope as God hopes.

I am trying to learn how to express a revolutionary or radical type of Godly love to everyone who crosses my path. If we live in love, we can create the conditions for having an abundant life. God is love and loves us radically. To ignite that fire within, we just have to do our job regardless of what others do -- our job is to love others unconditionally!

Love is the very best gift we can give to God, and to others.

Jesus says, "A new commandment I give to you, that you love one another, as I have loved you, that you love one another. By this all will know that you are My disciples, if you have love for one another" (John 13:34). To be His disciple, then, we should love others. These are very specific and clear instructions but many will try to parse or dissect this scripture in order to look for loopholes or work-arounds. God is not looking for people to work-around His laws; His law is not to be worked around. I had to surrender my will in order to do God's will. I had to totally flip the way I viewed the world and just let it go. 'Not my way but His way,' had to be my new internal directive. Jesus gave us this internal directive and too many believers neglect to follow it.

Love does not look for offense but looks to forgive. The forgiveness doesn't have anything to do with how we feel because it's an act of faith and is based upon obedience to God. God says that if we do not forgive others, He will not forgive us. Many people say, 'I may forgive but I won't forget.' That is not the right kind of forgiveness or love that Jesus speaks about. We are to forgive because God forgives us. Forgiveness is based on love. We can't say we have love when we still hold grudges or resentments or bitterness or anger against others. None of these emotions please God nor do they allow our requests to be granted. If your life is not what you want it to be, look at the love inside of you. The lack of love inside us opens the door for the devil and keeps our prayers from being answered. So many people cannot give love because they do not understand what it means to love in a healthy manner. I used to be like that but now know a better way. Love is unselfish and does not behave rudely or badly. Love forgives completely. Love has no guile, love is selfless. Love is not jealous or proud. Paul wrote in 1 Corinthians 13, how loves "beareth all things, believeth all things, hopeth all things, endureth all things." Do you love in this manner?

I did not but I now strive to develop my capacity to love each day, not in word but in deed. I had to learn how to love and how to develop the ability to love with my whole heart. Whenever you find yourself stumbling into anger or envy or greed or any other sin, check your love gauge. "He that loves his brother abides in the light and there is none occasion of stumbling in Him (1 John 2:10)." Love by definition is the light. Love is whole and healthy. Love seeks to look for the little bit of God in everyone. Love wants to share what it has with the world because it is pure.

Competition is not part of love. Many people unfortunately know only dysfunctional love. Challenge your current definition of love. Love is the ultimate power in the universe. God is light and love! God is limitless; thus, love is limitless. God made us and breathed breath into us. Love creates possibilities. With love in my heart, I became the richest man in the world because of the joy inside of me which came from love.

The Bible says in Matthew 5:44-45, "Love your enemies and bless those who curse you, do good to them that hate you and pray for them which despitefully use you, and persecute you..." I am better at this now because of the love I have for God. I still have a ways to go but I'm living intentionally now. Love for God must come first in every believer's life. If we love God with all our heart, soul, mind, and strength, then loving others and ourselves is easy. We were created by a loving and merciful God. Love is all encompassing and it wants the best for others. Love wants others to grow and become more. Become a living example of love. Our love for God is expressed through how we treat others.

Each interaction with others should be seen as an encounter with another one of God's creations. God loves others as He loves you. If someone you know falls short and treats you poorly, help to show them the light. Help that person to know love through your actions. The Bible says that we should not fight evil with evil, but with good. We are all responsible for how we choose to act, we can show love or not. God says in His word that He is not to be mocked. In that, we sow what we reap (Galatians 6:7-8). If we can focus on developing and putting out love then love is what we will receive in return.

'Know Better' Empowerment Exercise: Choose to see the love in everyone. Choose to see the beauty in everyone.

Love will elevate your life. Do everything with love because love vibrates at a higher frequency than any other force in the universe. If you operate your business or any other endeavor with love as your guiding force, it has no choice but to succeed.

Love wants others to fly high even if you can't fly yourself. Love is focused on helping others see the light. I would be so happy if everyone in my life becomes something more/greater with God at their center. Love can heal us. Love can move us to do great things for God. God wants us to expand who we are and love a lot more. Loving with my whole heart is my goal now.

Love can be developed. Some people are so caught up in what they do for a living. Whatever you do is not important because it's not who we are that is important; it is who we are becoming. Who are you becoming each day?

Love creates possibilities: If we strive to be love, doors will open up in ways we could never have imagined. The world is one of wonder, powered by light and love.

Ralph Waldo Emerson said, *"Love is our highest word and the synonym for God."*

If we all work to show people the beautiful nature of an all-consuming love expressed in a healthy manner, then the ills of the world would be healed. If we have hate in our hearts it takes up space inside of us that could be used for love. If we have unforgiveness in our hearts it takes up more space that could be used for love. Love frees us to do more. Love allows us to be more than we are.

Inspiration comes from love. Unconditional love and loving with our whole heart empowers us to do things that we could never have previously imagined. I could have never imagined that I would be writing a book such as this but it's all about God and sharing what He has given me. When you release love into a problem, you release God. The world is bright and one of infinite possibilities when love is at our core.

There is the old parable that says there are two wolves inside of us, one of light and one of darkness. Which one will you choose to guide you? It's the one we feed each day that will show us the path. Demons can only grow in hearts without love. The demons can only win if we feed them but if we pour in light be doing uplifting things and maintaining daily positive rituals then the darkness cannot get in.

By walking in love, success will emerge!

Love heals. Love changes our very nature and redeems us. Love connects us to God and allows us to listen to that still voice of God. It was love that caused Jesus to lay down His life for us. "And what this love consists in is this: that we live and walk in accordance with and guided by

His commandments. This is the commandment, as you have heard from the beginning, that you continue to walk in love (2 John 6)."

If you want abundance in your life, first want it for others (an expression of love); and if you want happiness in your life, then want it for others first (another expression of love). If we all allow God's love to flow through us and in us, we will live a truly extraordinary life. You will be able to move from a life of suffering to light, once you open up your core to love. Light begets light. Love begets love.

Johann Wolfgang von Goethe said, *"Light, light, the world needs more light."*

Love cannot live alongside pride, ego, bitterness, anger, hatred, envy and other negative forces. Commit to love completely, love with your whole heart; and your life will explode with blessings and abundance. Love is the real secret to success. The Bible says love never fails. If you love God, then love is not an option. Love honors God!

"When I opened my heart and started to love everyone around me with my whole heart, I felt peace for the first time in my life." Philip Allan Turner

I wanted to finish this step with a few quotes:

"Love many things, for there lies the true strength, and whosoever loves much performs much, and can accomplish much, and what is done in love is done well." Vincent Van Gogh

"Hatred paralyzes life; love releases it. Hatred confuses life; love harmonizes it. Hatred darkens life; love illuminates it." Martin Luther King

"Hate is not conquered by hate. Hate is conquered by love. This is the law eternal." Gautama Siddhartha (the Buddha).

"As love grows in you, beauty grows too. For love is the beauty of the soul." St. Augustine of Hippo.

"There is no difficulty that enough love will not conquer...

No door that enough love will not open

No gulf that enough love will not bridge,

No wall that enough love will not throw down...

It makes no difference how deeply seated may be the trouble,

How great the mistake,

Sufficient realization of love will resolve it all.

If only you could love enough,

You would be the happiest and most powerful being in the universe." Emmet Fox

"Every day we can choose to live a life centered on love because there is no limit to the amount of love the human heart can hold." Philip Allan Turner

'Know Better' Life Principle: ***Make your life story, a love story.***

Chapter 13

Step Eleven: *Forgive everyone especially yourself. Eject any ill will or negative bias you have towards anyone in your life.*

The last step discussed love and it's connected to this step. Love is all-encompassing and includes forgiveness. Unforgiveness is like a cancer inside of us because it causes others ills within us. Untreated cancer spreads throughout the body and starts to kill other systems after it kills the initial organ. Unforgiveness acts in the same way because it spreads and starts to negatively affect other areas of the body, mind and spirit. A lack of forgiveness is a darkness which can cause all types of physical ailments because these resentments create negative energy inside. Negative energy interferes with our communication with God and limits our infinite potential.

We should all strive to live by doing small things with great love. If we love deeply then we will forgive. Love creates huge spiritual energy around you. We are commanded to love God and our neighbor as well (Mathew 22:38-40), both on the same level. Our efforts to love our neighbor must be equal to our efforts to love for God. Mother Teresa discussed how we can have joy, when our heart burns with love. Jesus tells us to love others as He loved us (John 13:34). Jesus gave up his life because of the love He had for us.

Mother Teresa has stated several maxims for a spiritual life to include *"Don't be afraid to love each other."* She also explained how we can see God, *"To be able to see God in the silence of our hearts, we need a pure heart. A pure heart only can see God; can understand what He speaks to us."* Our hearts can only be pure if it's filled with love and forgiveness. A heart with unforgiveness is not pure and does not honor God.

This is a very simple step which some people make very complicated. Forgiveness frees us and releases positive energy into the Universe. 'Letting go' not only frees our energy but our attention as well. I know whenever I had a grudge against someone before I had an awakening, I would think bad things about that person many times throughout the week. I dwelled on the negative and only wished the worse for them. But, I forgave everyone and with that forgiveness brought much more emotional space for other positive and loving thoughts. Unforgiveness takes up emotional space for other things. Once the baggage of the past is thrown out then it's easy to channel your inner power into other areas.

'Know Better' Life Question: Are there still people you haven't forgiven or holding grudges against? Do yourself a favor, and forgive.

I believe the most beautiful example of forgiveness is when Jesus was on the cross. Luke 23:32-34 explains the act of forgiveness very simply. "There were also two others, criminals, led with him to be put to death. And when they had come to the place called Calvary, there they crucified Him and the criminals, one on the right hand and the other on the left. Then Jesus said, "Father forgive them, for they do not know what they do..." Most people do not know what they do because they just act unconsciously reacting to external stimuli like cattle or sheep.

The most famous comment on forgiving is from the Gospel of Mathew 6:14-15, "If you forgive men their trespasses, your heavenly Father will also forgive you. But if you do not forgive men their trespasses, neither will your Father forgive your trespasses."

Later in Mathew 18:21-22, "Then Peter came to Him and said, 'Lord, how often shall my brother sin against me, and I forgive him? Up to seven times?' Jesus said to him, 'I do not say to you, up to seven time, but up to seventy times seven."

There are some who would start to count how many times they have forgiven someone but they do not understand the spirit of what Jesus was trying to say. It goes back to what was said in the earlier verse where it states that we will not be forgiven if we do not forgive. Too many people spend too much energy trying not to do the right thing. Forgiving is good for our health as it relaxes us. I forgave everyone which ever wronged me and prayed that God draws them closer as He drew me closer to me. I pray that they are blessed. I left all my negative bias behind. Forgive, so you can be forgiven.

In Colossians 3:13, we learn that we should, "Bear with one another, forgiving one another, if anyone has a complaint against another; even as Christ forgave you, so you also must do."

According to the writer of Proverbs, conduct is the best indicator of character. If someone says that he or she is a Godly person, their words can only be proven by consistent actions (Proverbs 20:11). Appearance and words are deceiving; behavior is the best judge of character. The Bible says that their (people) lips say they love Me (God), but their hearts are far from Me (God). Forgiveness is a commandment from God and our actions will show if we truly love do because God says, "if you love me, you will keep my commandments." As followers of Jesus, we demonstrate our love for Him by what we do, not just what we say.

May our devotion to God, because of His love for us, be revealed in our actions each day.

This goes back to my belief that it's easy but we make it hard. We humans make life so hard for ourselves. I know I did before I gained more perspective. I realized that I just need to do my job and honor God through my actions. Forgiving honors God. I strive each day to add more light into the world and less chaos. I need to be a part of the solution in every aspect of my life.

Hebrew 10:30 states, "For we know Him who said, 'Vengeance is Mine, I will repay,' says the Lord. And again, the Lord will judge His people." Our job is to serve God, love others and forgive others regardless of what others may do to us.

One of my favorite verses come from the Apostle Paul who wrote in Philippians 3:13-14, "Brethren, I do not count myself to have apprehended; but one thing I do, forgetting those things which are behind and reaching forward to those things which are ahead, I press towards the goal for the prize of the upward call of God in Christ Jesus."

We have to eject all the past baggage, hurts and disappointments so that we can be the people who God intended us to be. I want all of us to know better and do better. Unforgiveness creates negative conditions in us and separates us from God. Unforgiveness leads to bitterness and resentment. Once that root of bitterness becomes deeply entrenched inside, it starts twisting around and strangling our hearts. When the heart begins to be strangled then it's tough for love to flourish inside. It's the same when we are choking; it's difficult for air to come into our lungs. Cleaning out our hearts allow love to flow inside which creates the conditions to have an abundant life. We have the power to live any type of life we choose to live. I say this statement because we create either positive or negative circumstances for ourselves by the state of our heart. If we fill our hearts with bitterness and unforgiveness then it takes away space which could be filled with love.

Some people are addicted to their pain but God does not want us to live that way. This is why the above verses on forgiveness are repeated so many times in the Bible because we humans are stubborn.

Eject any ill will or negative bias for anyone who has entered your life. Eject it, save yourself! Forgiveness is one of the highest forms of self-love, being good and gentle with oneself. T.D. Jakes states in his fabulous book, *Let It Go*, "*That the other insidious danger of not practicing forgiveness is that we become contagious carriers of the very offenses that we ourselves have suffered.*"

Letting go frees us of all that past negative energy and allows us to heal from the inside out. The body is amazing and can heal itself. Just read anything by Louise Hay especially her great work, *You Can Heal Your Life*, Louise Hay states, "*I am the star in my own movie. I am also the author and the director. I create wonderful roles for myself.*" We have the power inside of us. Louise Hay discusses how, "*we all need to do forgiveness work....One of the biggest spiritual lessons is to understand that everyone is doing the best they can at any given moment.*"

Some people hold grudges for years. Don't hold that negative energy inside of you, it only hurts you. If you want to realize your potential, then create a positive internal environment so that you can draw more positive energy into you.

The body can heal itself but we have to create the internal conditions to promote what we want on the outside. If we want to become whole, healthy and balanced then we have to work on the inside first. We have to fix our defective thinking because our thoughts leads to our feeling which lead to our actions. Once we fix our thinking errors; we can love and forgive others which allows us to tap into an inner strength which enables us to do more than thought we could ever do.

Love is the most powerful force in the universe because God is love. Forgiveness is a tangible act of love. Forgiving others honors God and glorifies God. The devil is waiting like a roaring lion for us to hate and hold grudges. The devil is patient and we must be vigilant each day to lean into the light.

What is the key to moving beyond the hurts of the past? It is loving above the sin or the offense. We need to love the person with our whole heart. We can hate the sin but we need to love the person because it is our reasonable service or duty to God. Everyone is just as broken or defective as we are but we can recover by becoming more self-aware and examining ourselves. We are all human and all make mistakes. Some people don't know what they are doing as they create paths of chaos in their wake. Being human means that we will make the wrong decisions at times but with wisdom and more perspective, we learn to make better decisions over time. The Bible is the closest operational manual we have in life.

We all make it up as we go along or learned through the programming and conditioning of the past. Some of us have decided to stop putting our hands repeated on the hot stove and expecting a different result. When I choose to give my life to God, I learned how to radically change my thinking and habits. I started doing different things in order to get a different result.

When we are hurt by others, we don't need to lash out or seek revenge. It's our ego and the devil who wants us to do lash out but God wants us to forgive and to love. Who will you serve today? We need to offer the other cheek of kindness and compassion because no one is perfect. Compassion is closely related to love and forgiveness. We cannot realistically be looking for inner happiness if we do not practice love, forgiveness and compassion on a daily basis.

In truth, no one has to live with anger. Living angry is a choice. Many people have decided to get beyond the hurt of the past. I heard a sermon by Joyce Meyer on forgiveness where she explained how she completely forgave her abuser, her father. She let it go and embraced forgiveness, so much so, that her father gave his life to Christ before he died. Loving our enemies is not just a New Testament commandment; it's one of the core beliefs of Christianity. Jesus explains in Mathew 5:44-45 that if someone is an enemy, we should love them. If they curse us, we should bless them. If they hate us, we should do only good to them. If our enemy goes out of his/her way to hurt us, we should respond by praying for them. God wants us to respond with love. Love is the path!

We should examine our hearts for bitterness. Unforgiveness is a negative seed which drowns out God's voice. To hear God's voice, we must create conditions in our hearts which are 'of God'. Everyone who has ever done me wrong, I forgive and pray blessings over their lives. God wants us all to love and forgive. Do yourself a favor, forgive and live the abundant life that God desires for you!

"To err is human, to forgive is divine." Alexander Pope (1711)

Mother Teresa stated, *"If we really want to love, we must learn how to forgive."*

"The weak can never forgive. Forgiveness is the attribute of the strong." Mahatma Gandhi

Chapter 14

Step Twelve: *Show compassion and kindness to everyone especially yourself.*

These steps were created for me and helped me perhaps they will help you too. I had to improve my inner voice, love myself, forgive myself and take off all self-imposed limitations on my life. I learned to be kind to myself 24 hours a day which includes making sure I created an internal photo of who I want to be and make a plan to achieve that photo. If we are honest with ourselves, we will see that we have not always been good or gentle with ourselves enough nor have we been always kind to others. We must be kind with ourselves in order to be good to ourselves.

"The Lord is gracious and full of compassion (Psalm 111:4)." The Bible speaks of God as the Father of compassion. Compassion is an emotion where we feel a loving response to others' pain or suffering which motivates us to help them. The Buddha stated, *"Compassion is that which makes the heart of the good move at the pain of others. It crushes and destroys the pain of others; thus, it is called compassion. It is called compassion because it shelters and embraces the distressed."*

The heart of Jesus is compassion, a divine passion! We need to have compassion in our everyday lives. In the Bible there is a story in the Gospel of Mark 1:40-45 where Divine compassion is seen. Jesus is moved with compassion, stretched out His hand and touched a leper. Jesus told the leper that He was willing to help him. At that time in Palestine, lepers were isolated from society and compelled to live alone. This particular leper threw himself at the feet of Jesus and said, "If you are willing, You can make me clean. Jesus was moved with compassion, touched the man and said, "I am willing; be cleansed." The leper was healed.

In another story in the Bible which starts in Exodus 33:18. Moses asked to see God's glory or goodness. God tells Moses that, "I will make all My goodness pass before you, and I will proclaim the name of the Lord before you. I will be gracious to whom I will be gracious, and I will have compassion on whom I will have compassion." God goes on to let Moses see his back as it was not possible for any man to see God's face and live. This story describes God's compassion for his faithful servant.

In the Gospel of Luke 7:13, we see another example when Jesus comes to the gates of the city of Nain. Jesus saw a dead man being "carried out, the only son of his mother, and she was a widow... When the Lord saw her, He had compassion on her and said to her, 'Do not weep.' Then He came and touched the open coffin, and those who carried him stood still. And He said, 'Young man, I say to you arise.' So he who was dead sat up and began to speak." The mother's tears moved Jesus and He showed compassion. Jesus cares for us and wants to help us. We must first help ourselves first.

Always strive to be more Christ-like, aiming to be better each day.

In 2 Corinthians 1:3-7 states "Praise be to the God and Father of our Lord Jesus Christ, the father of compassion and the God of all comfort, who comforts us in all our troubles, so that we can comfort those in any trouble with the comfort we ourselves from God. For just as the sufferings of Christ flow over into our lives, so also through Christ our comfort overflows. If we are distressed, it is for your comfort and salvation; if we are comforted, it is for your comfort, which produces in you patient endurance of the same sufferings we suffer. And our hope for you is firm, because we know that just as you share in our sufferings, so also you share in our comfort."

I made Jesus Christ my life coach and He challenges me to forsake my own desires and treat others with love and compassion. When I started living this way, the quality of my life improved greatly. Every day I strive to treat others with compassion.

'Know Better' Life Principle: **Compassion is centered on living with passion to love others.**

Other spiritual traditions also discuss the concept of compassion. The Dalai Lama XIV has said, *'if you want others to be happy, practice compassion. If you want to be happy, practice compassion."* Loving-kindness and compassion can be cultivated each day.

In learning to love and forgive, I came to believe that compassion went along with the two other qualities. Once we start to live with love at our core, it provides a path to those who are lost. God has asked us to love, forgive and to show compassion. God never gives us a command without giving us grace and strength to obey.

The power is inside of us. Ephesians 4:32, "Be kind and compassionate to one another, forgiving each other, just as Christ God forgave you." These principles seemed easier and clearer to understand to me once I opened my heart and mind. I learned that God was compassionate and thus we should strive to be like Him in our conduct. A kind word, a smile, a loving hug or kiss, any gesture of kindness shows others that we have love in us.

"But the fruit of the Spirit is love, joy, peace, long-suffering, kindness, goodness, faithfulness (Galatians 5:22)." I never knew that there was an eternal blueprint out there before reading the Bible and other spiritual texts. We are told in the Bible in Ephesians 5:1-2 that we should, "Be imitators of God... and walk in Love." Once I started walking with God, each day my spirit became stronger as it reached new heights found in becoming one with God and love. Loving others allowed me to reach out with kindness and compassion to everyone.

In Mark 7:6, there are some more powerful words I came to internalize, "...this people honors Me with their lips, but their heart is far from me." There are people who praise God for an hour or two a week but the real test occurs outside of church or the worship hall or the mosque. Changing our facial expression is easier than changing our inner attitude, but true worship requires that our thoughts, words, and spirit all show that we are a true follower of the one true source of Divine Power in the universe, God.

"The world is the embodiment of Divine Love. All created things are its material expression. If you can once rouse yourself to that Divine Love, you will see everywhere in this universe only the play of the One. Isolating himself from the Divine Love, man fumbles about and misses the real import of life." AnandaMayi Ma, an Indian saint.

Many people understand that we should show love, compassion and kindness but still do not act in this manner. There is a Chinese quote I love, *"To know and yet not to do, is in fact not to know."* Wang Yang Ming

We know that we should show more love to others, what's stopping us from doing it each day?We should "be doers of the Word" as James stated in 1:22. James provided such great advice on how to live. The same can be said for John as well, "By this all will know that you are My disciples, if you have love for one another. (John 13:35)." If we love, show compassion and kindness to everyone then we are connecting to the infinite power of the universe.

There is an anonymous poem I love:

> *"You are called with a holy calling,*
>
> *The light of the world to be;*
>
> *To lift up the lamp of the Gospel,*
>
> *That others the light may see."*

Mother Teresa explained that kindness communicates love. She told her fellow missionaries that they should, *"Be the living expression of God's kindness: kindness in your face, kindness in your eyes, kindness in your smile, kindness in your warm greeting. In the slums we are the light of God' kindness to the poor."* I studied Mother Teresa because she was kindness and love. She believed that spreading Christ's love was the main goal everywhere she went. She showed deep love and compassion for everyone she saw. I came to view her as an example to strive for.

Albert Einstein explained, *"Our task must be to free ourselves from this prison by widening our circle of compassion to embrace all living creatures and the whole of nature in its beauty."* Einstein believed that we lived in a kind of prison of delusions which restricted our thinking.

Ephesians 5:19 states that we should, "Speak to one another in psalms and hymns and spiritual songs." Uplifting others with our words should be our daily goal. I learned much from the Apostle Paul especially through his letters he wrote in a Roman prison. In Ephesians 4:1-2, Paul wrote, "I therefore, the prisoner of the Lord, beseech you to walk worthy of the calling with which you were called. Be humble, be gentle, be patient bearing with one another in love." Paul wrote from prison not knowing whether he would be freed or killed. I came to view Paul as one of my Biblical heroes because he was steadfast and chose to be a light in the world.

Fill your heart with the beauty of God's word. Clean out your heart to the core and then leave the door open for all to see.

Colossians 3:12 states, "As the elect of God, holy and beloved, put on tender mercies, kindness...longsuffering." Several verse later we learn, "Let the word of Christ dwell in you richly in all wisdom, teaching and admonishing one another in psalms and hymns and spiritual songs. (Colossians 3:16). The Bible provides such rich examples on what is pleasing to God. David in Psalm 19:14 wrote, "Let the words of my mouth and the meditation of my heart be acceptable in Your sight, O Lord." We should keep our hearts pure and open so God can use us in a mighty way.

Today, I strive to be a light to all. I use 1 Timothy 4:12 as a life verse: "Be an example to the believers in word, in conduct, in love, in spirit, in faith, in purity."

So much of what we do affects us on the inside. How we think, what we say and what we put in our hearts affect our quality of life. "A merry heart does good, like medicine (Proverbs 17:22)." Showing kindness and compassion helps us just as much as the other person. Having a smile and accepting people for who they are heals our hearts and brings inner peace.

James gives us practical advice, "Be swift to hear, slow to speak, slow to wrath... (James 1:19)." We should help others by showing kindness and compassion everywhere we go. Being kind and showing compassion is an important concept to internalize. It's critical to do this if we want to have inner peace and ignite that inner fire. Another aspect is to make sure that we are kind and show compassion to ourselves on a daily basis.

In this vein, I wanted to discuss another aspect of this step, being compassionate to ourselves because we will not always do the right thing. Sometimes we will fall down and miss the mark but we must pick up ourselves and keep moving forward by showing compassion to ourselves. Many people are kind and compassionate to others but beat themselves up as a routine. We should show kindness and compassion to ourselves in all things. This does not mean that we should not hold ourselves accountable but that when we make a mistake, but instead look for the lesson and then move on. It's through these missteps that we grow and learn. As a child, once we put our hands on a hot stove the first time, we never did it again because we learned the lesson through the pain.

One of the keys to this spiritual plan is to see the lesson the first time and try not to touch that hot stove again. Learn the lesson, be good to yourself and move on in order to do it better the next time. It's okay to take one step sideways from time to time or take three steps forward and one step backwards, this is part of the process of learning.

The process is important and should be respected. Failure helps to get us to our future objective in a better way. Once you fall down, brush off the dust and see it as a teachable moment. Get up and move on without judging yourself or invalidating yourself with negative self-talk. One of the most important points is to learn the lesson in the mistake so we can grow into the people God wants us to be. In Mathew 10:14, Jesus tells his disciples when they minister in a new city and their words are not received, 'to shake off the dust from your feet,' before moving forward. There are times in life when we will fail at things, and we should be compassionate with ourselves and shake off the pain in order to move forward.

Many people are driven by their demons because of the conditioning of the past. We need to recalibrate our lives along a more whole and healthy spiritual paradigm. In order to find one's purpose in life, we need to see what has been the driving force in our lives previously. Our beliefs create our world view, which leads to our actions. Many people do not understand how unkind they are to themselves as well as to other people. There are people whose normal operating directive is negative; negativity to themselves and others. This 20 step plan is about restructuring our thoughts and recalibrating our hearts to silent that inner critic.

We are not our past but whomever we decide to be in the present. If you can identify how you have been operating in the past then you can change your habits and behaviors. It's okay to say, "I have been a negative person but today I will make a plan to change myself on the inside to live an abundantly positive life." This is about an honest assessment which will lead to a better life.

'Know Better' Empowerment Exercise: Evaluate what you say to yourself and others throughout the day. Keep a log for one day so that you are able to analyze it accurately. A though/word/deed log for one day can help us understand what we say each day. Once you realize what you do subconsciously by habit--you can change it.

There are some people who are "haters." These unfortunate souls do not understand that they are using mental space to keep love out. These individuals are purposely limiting their blessings. Their potential is limited because they are focusing their energy in negative directions instead of positive. Those who hate will always find it difficult to connect to that all powerful universal positive energy.

On the other hand, there are people who love, show kindness and compassion in everything they do. These fortunate people have learned a valuable secret in life. We reap what we sow. If we uplift our thoughts and actions then we will receive the same in return. The law of attraction works whether we realize it or not. Ronda Byrne explained the law of attraction in her excellent book, *The Secret*.

The Bible says that God desires that none should perish. I want everyone to gain the inner peace that I have found. "Indeed, we count them blessed who endure. You have heard of the perseverance of Job and seen the end intended by the Lord--that the Lord is very compassionate and merciful (James 5:11)."

"Finally, all of you be of one mind, having compassion for one another, love as brothers, be tenderhearted, be courteous; not returning evil for evil or reviling for reviling, but on the contrary blessing, knowing that you were called to this, that you may inherit a blessing (1 Peter 3:8-17)."

"Compassion is a verb." Thich Nhat Hanh

Chapter 15

Step Thirteen: *Do not judge anyone especially yourself. Leave judgment to God. With all of our faults and the mistakes we make as humans, we are in no position to judge anyone else.*

We judge as a way to make ourselves feel better but that is not real, that's an illusion. Inner peace can come if we have honest intentions and live in the light. Judging others is one of those negative forces which don't help us to grow. There are times when we judge and don't even know all the facts but our natural mind loves to jump to negative conclusions.

Jesus said in Luke 6:37, "Judge not, and you shall not be judged. Condemn not, and you shall not be condemned. Forgive and you shall be forgiven." Several verses later, Jesus says, "A disciple is not above his teacher, but everyone who is perfectly trained will be like his teacher. And why do you look at the speck in your brother's eye, but do not perceive the plank in your own eye? Or how can you say to your brother, 'Brother, let me remove the speck that is in your eye' when you yourself do not see the plank that is in your own eye? Hypocrite! First remove the plank from your own eye, and then you will see clearly to remove the speck that is in your brother's eye." Too many people are eager to point out faults in others while ignoring their own faults.

Today, I focus on removing the plank in my eye so I can move closer to God. I have lots of planks in my eye. A plank is a stronghold in your life or a weakness, foible, fault or other deficiency. I now focus on burning off those ungodly things in my heart which displeases God. I am striving, making an effort and working hard to change my thinking, speech and actions so that I can be a living testimony to the redemptive power of God's love. I am not judging others but instead I am tending to my own garden. I am working on my side of the street and dealing with my own issues so I can be whole and healthy. My focus is my inner world so that I can be a light in this world.

The plank will always cause us problems especially since the devil knows our weaknesses. The devil wants us to not focus on our own issues, but instead on the issues of our neighbors, co-workers, spouses, or relatives. If we work each day to develop the inner person, more blessings will flow into our lives. God wants to help us to truly be His children in every sense.

<u>**'Know Better' Life Question**</u>: Are there any planks in your eye that you need to tend to? Who are we to judge others?

Mathew 7:1 states, "Judge not, that you be not judged. For with what judgment you judge, you will be judged, and with the measure you use, it will be measured back to you." My life became

so much simpler when I stop resisting and surrendered to a higher law. God's instructions are clear but our complicated minds want to look for loopholes.

God is the judge, not us. Who are we to put our faulty views on others? James, Jesus' half brother, said it so simply, "Do not speak evil of one another, brethren. He who speaks evil of a brother and judges his brother, speaks evil of the law and judges the law. But if you judge the law, you are not a doer of the law but a judge. There is one Lawgiver (another translations uses the word - Judge), who is able to save and to destroy."

'Know Better' Life Principle: **Stay Teachable.**

An old man once gave me some great advice - always stay teachable. Being teachable is about looking for the wisdom or lesson in every situation without judgment. I learned by working my 20 steps that once I started loving, showing kindness, compassion and forgiving, I stopped judging so much. Like most people, I used to judge everything and everyone. I judged how you looked, talked, walked and worked. I was able to overcome this by examining myself through working my 20 steps.

2 Timothy 4:8 states, "Finally, there is laid up for me the crown of righteousness, which the Lord, the righteous judge, will give to me on that Day, and not only to me but also to all who have loved His appearing." God is the judge.

The Apostle Paul wrote in Romans 14:13, "Therefore let us not judge one another anymore, but rather resolve this, not to put a stumbling block or a cause to fall in our brother's way." Judging creates stumbling blocks because we are setting ourselves apart from our fellow human. My goal now is to put light into the world and I realized that judging others was not doing that. The more positive effort I put into learning about myself and changing my negative habits, I started to feel real inner joy. The energy we use to point fingers at others can be used for more positive endeavors. Every action we take either puts positive or negative energy into the universe. But by doing our job which is serving God and doing what is pleasing to Him, we can add positive energy into this world. What we put into the universe, we get back. We sow what we reap.

In Zen Buddhism there is a saying that says, "*Do not think that the knowledge you presently possess is changeless, absolute truth. Avoid being narrow-minded and bound to present views. Learn and practice nonattachment from views in order to be open to receive others viewpoints.*"

Many times we judge because we feel we are right and our ego wishes to be fed by saying that we are right and others are wrong. The ego feeds our need to judge. The ego wants to be right and point out the faults of others while not wanting to look at its own faults and foibles. In John 8:7, Jesus said, "He without sin among you, let him cast the stone at her first." We all fall short of the glory of God and all sin according to the Bible. We all have internal work to do on the inside. The devil loves when we judge others instead of loving others. Judging creates discord and chaos inside of us as well.

Any negativity we put into the world will be returned to us, just as any positive energy we put into the world will be returned as well. We can change the conditions surrounding us, by changing what we do each day. Judging is a negative energy force which interferes with our overall internal energy. Positive energy activities empowers us and negative energy activities weakens us.

Another aspect of this step is not to judge yourself too harshly in life. Learn the lesson of what God is trying to show you and then move on. This is part being good to ourselves. Working the other steps which involves loving yourself and changing your inner dialogue to be always positive will help to work this step. It's okay to honestly analyze your thoughts or actions but it should always be with self-love, not self-loathing.

Not judging anyone else is also centered on working on our side of the street, following our own path in life. We all need to work to become better people on the inside by running our own race. Hebrews 12:1 states, "Therefore we also, since we are surrounded by so great a cloud of witnesses, let us lay aside every weight, and the sin which so easily snares us, and let us run with endurance the race that is set before us." If we all focus on becoming better than our situations will get better.

Many people have been conditioned to feel good by talking negatively about others. Once you start to speak negatively about people, you are judging their actions. In my faith as a Christian, we are always told to hate the sin but love the sinner; this is very difficult for people to do. I believe by taking steps, we can grow and become the people who God wants us to be.

'Know Better' Empowerment Exercise: Next time you have a negative thought about someone---Immediately pray for them and ask God to bless them. Pray that God draws that person closer to Him as He has brought you closer to Him. Make this your new routine.

Judging is about the ego and its need to feel superior. The ego desires to make you feel good based on illusions. We have been conditioned to feed the ego and the ego wants to protect itself. The ego contributes to living a dysfunctional life. The ego wants to point fingers at others. The ego loves to criticize and judge maliciously anyone crossing its path. The ego wants to tell you that you are better than everyone else. Many people are addicted to criticizing others. They don't know that their conditioning has put them on this negative track, making it necessary to put down others in their mind in order to feel good about themselves. The ego looks to strengthen itself by looking for faults in other people. The ego says: "You're stupid and I'm smart; you're ugly and I'm better looking; you're broke and I have more money than you; you're fat but I'm thinner, you're trash and I'm better than you." The ego loves these statements and believes that it's taking care of you but this is dysfunctional thinking. You will never be whole giving in to these thoughts. Make a decision to pray for all those who are still in the darkness.

The ego is always looking to feed its dysfunctional view of the world and enhance its artificial sense of self. Most people who live an ego-based existence are constantly looking to enhance their mental image of themselves. But the ego-centered view is an illusion and is not healthy in the long term. We create this self-image and attempt to justify it throughout our lives by criticizing others. The ego prefers to judge by saying on the inside, "See, look at them, they are trash. I'm better than they are." If you focus on strengthening the inside then all will be well.

As long as you continue to judge or allow your inner dialogue to criticize others, you will stay in the darkness. True light and love will elude you when the ego directs your life. Once out of the darkness and conscious of how your mind works, you can move beyond the ego to a healthy place. To awaken, we must replace the former (ego) with something whole and healthy (a solid spiritual foundation). Once you recognize that it's the ego feeding your need to judge others, and then you can change your behavior.

The ego thrives on drama and chaos. "Feed me", the ego says or you will not be happy. This is a lie and another tool of the devil. The devil wants your energy to stay negative and at lower levels. The unfulfilled ego is another reason that most people are unhappy. In creating the 20 steps, I became aware of my thoughts and how my ego led my actions in the past. Judging, criticizing and putting others down takes up mental space and emanates negative energy into the universe. Every time, we put negative energy into the universe, we are ensuring that more negative energy will return into our lives.

We can stop judging others because we are good in the eyes of God. God loves you just as you are! If I can sum up all my steps in one word, it's focused on the love of God, self and others. Loving yourself is being good to you and judging others is not healthy. We just have to do our job and work on ourselves. In the Bible in Luke 6:43 it says, a tree shall be known by its fruit. Once again, I ask you to search your behavior to see whether your behavior uplifts others or not?

The Bible also discusses following the spirit of truth. "The Spirit of Truth, whom the world cannot receive, because it neither sees Him nor knows Him; but you know Him, for He dwells with you and will be in you (John 14:17)." God is in us and the potential for great growth is available for those who want it. There is a higher standard that each of us should hold ourselves to. We can do this by doing internal self-diagnostics routinely (centered on love) in order to stay awake and conscious. The ego will continue to look for ways to be fed. The ego will find new and creative ways to take back control over your life. We must be constantly vigilant taking our pulse frequently to make sure that we are not falling back into our old ways.

Stop looking for loopholes to being a better person. We must all put the work in to be better. Change is necessary and it's difficult at times. My ego constantly is waiting to take over. My ego wants to jump to conclusions and tell others what they are wrong. The ego is cunning. Don't let your ego control your life because your ego does not want you to be happy. The dysfunctional ego wants disagreements and augments. I mentioned earlier that the ego stands for easing or edging God out.

The only way to eliminate the ego is to increase our spiritual and meditative practices. These practices will ease the ego out and allow a healthier new internal operating directive to take its place. Too many people are outwardly motivated instead of being inwardly focused. As long as the ego is in charge, this will never change. But once we fall in love with our higher power, then we will be motivated to change.

The Bible and other great spiritual books provide guidance on how to be a better, more fulfilled person. You can attempt to do it your way but, most likely, you will continue to get what you have gotten until you radically change something. John 15:11 provides some insight from Jesus, "These things I have spoken to you, that My joy may remain you, and that your joy may be full." God does not want us to suffer, whether you follow my inspirational plan for joy or another person's plan, please strive to have a life filled with love, joy and purpose.

1 Thessalonians 5:16 states, "Rejoice always." I have joy in my heart because I have tamed my ego and make an effort every moment of the day to not judge or criticize others. I now focus on having joy always and putting out positive energy into the universe.

"Who are you to judge the life I live? I know I'm not perfect – and I don't live to be – but before you start pointing fingers...make sure your hands are clean!" Bob Marley

"Everyone is a genius. But if you judge a fish on its ability to climb a tree, it will live its whole life believing it's stupid." Albert Einstein

"Before you judge me, take my shoes and go through my way, try my tears, feel my pain, bump into each stone, which I stumbled on...And only then tell me that you know how to live." Adele, Grammy winning singer

Chapter 16

Step Fourteen: *Be thankful for all that is in your life. Be grateful! Having a loving heart also includes having a thankful heart. Gratitude opens up the doors of infinite power in your life.*

Gratitude channels positive energy into the Universe which in turn brings more joy into our lives. Gratitude is one of those positive emotional states with a higher level of energy. Higher levels of energy will always make us feel better. Love is the highest form of energy which is why it makes us feel strong and content. Gratitude brings out the same type of positive feelings into our lives.

Being thankful for all things in your life will open up a wave of positive energy. "In everything give thanks (1 Thessalonians 5:18)." Why does the Bible, the Torah, the Qur'an all express the need for us to be thankful at all times. In the Bible, God challenges us to always be thankful. He knows that it will be a challenge for us because as humans it's so easy to stay bound by our delusions, desires and hurts of the past to not see the beauty of the day. The devil loves when we are not thankful.

"As we express our gratitude, we must never forget that the highest appreciation is not to utter words, but to live by them." John F. Kennedy

There is no getting around it, God want us to be thankful in all circumstances. God wants us to pray with thanksgiving even though the future is uncertain. David provides amazing, insightful advice and wisdom in his Psalms. For example, Psalm 30:11-12 states, "You have turned for me my mourning into dancing; You have put off my sackcloth and clothed me with gladness, To the end that my glory may sing to You and not be silent. O Lord my God, I will give thanks to You forever." I found that when I was at my lowest point that when I thanked God for what I had, I felt better. Gratitude can help you rise above your circumstances.

In creating my steps, I learned that I must be steadfast in doing all of them. I made my steps for me but when I started speaking about them to the others, I found that others got a lot out of it. I have to work my steps on a daily basis through the heartbreaks and the pains.

Pain is important because it make us into better, stronger people. It's hard to thankful in difficult times but we can build those muscles. In dark times, be more thankful. Daniel "prayed and gave thanks" (Daniel 6:10) knowing that his life was in mortal danger in the lion's den. Gratitude can lead to amazing things.

I came to love a poem from Elizabeth Barrett Browning about thanking God:

I praise Thee while my days go on;
I love Thee while my days go on:
Through dark and dearth, through fire and frost,
With emptied arms and treasure lost, I thank Thee while my days go on.

Charles Spurgeon provides some great insight in the below quote:

"I bear willing witness that I owe more to the fire, and the hammer, and the file, than to anything else in my Lord's workshop. I sometimes question whether I have ever learned anything except through the rod. When my schoolroom is darkened, I see most."

I learned that it was not only about being grateful but also praising God during the hard times. The hard times are for our benefit because it shows us things that we would otherwise not perceive. We must praise and worship God at all times. Praise is another element of being thankful because it puts positive energy in universe. Praise is the outward expression of showing and living with gratitude in your heart. I praise God every day, throughout the day. It's hard to complain when you are being thankful. You can praise yourself out of a bad situation.

What is the opposite of being thankful and showing gratitude--complaining. Complaining and gratitude are opposite muscle groups. Sadness and gratitude is not compatible either. I want everyone to know that they have the inner power to positively affect their outer circumstances. Complaining is negative and puts negative energy into the universe. When we complain, we spit in God's face. Complaining is expressing the following, "God, what you are doing right now? I know better than you God." Complaining is one of ultimate insults to God. God sees the road ahead while we can only see a few feet ahead of us. Sometimes what we may think is a curse is a blessing and could actually save our lives. I praise His name and thank Him for all that have come into my life.

The Bible says in Joshua 1:9, "Have I not commanded you? Be strong and of good courage; do not be afraid, nor be dismayed, for the Lord your God is with you wherever you go." We shall be known by our actions, James, Jesus half-brother, says.

Sometimes, a person has been down for so long, it's a real challenge to get up. A new life can start with very small steps. Gratitude can be one of those steps. You can change your inner and outer dialogue with a small pivot. Wake up and tell God thank you every morning. It's my hope that grace and peace abound in you; and gratitude will help you on your journey.

'Know Better' Life Question: Do your actions say you are thankful and trust God or distrustful of God?

Psalm 100 is a psalm of thanksgiving. Write it down and carry it with you. Read it often.

Make a joyful shout to the Lord, all you lands!
Serve the Lord with gladness;

Come before His presence with singing.
Know that the Lord, He is God;
It is He who has made us, and not we ourselves;
We are His people and the sheep of His pasture.
Enter into His gates with thanksgiving,
And into His courts with praise.
Be thankful to Him, and bless his name.
For the Lord is good.
His mercy is everlasting,
And His truth endures to all generations.

When I decided to start this step, it was Psalm 100 that came to me. All of the major religions promote gratitude. Praise opens doors along with gratitude!

The Prophet Muhammad, founder of Islam, explained, "*Gratitude for the abundance you have received is the best insurance that the abundance will continue.*"

In the Qur'an 7:144, "*So hold that which I have given you and be of the grateful.*"

The Apostle Paul was in a Roman prison and was grateful. Paul explained in Philippians 4:6, "Be anxious for nothing, but in everything by prayer and supplication, with thanksgiving, let your request be made known to God." All the power we will ever need to channel is inside of us but there are some things required of us. Paul realized that he had the conditions for his own happiness even in prison.

'Know Better' Empowerment Exercise: Say thank you 100 times a day. Make a gratitude list of ten things daily.

Albert Einstein had a great quote: "*A hundred times every day I remind myself that my inner and outer life depend on the labors of other men, living and dead, and that I must exert myself in order to give in the same measure as I have received and am still receiving.*"

We should all be thankful each day for all that has come before, all that is here now and all that will come. Being grateful under any circumstance tells God that we trust Him unconditionally. Too many people are part-time worshippers. They praise God when good is in their life but waiver when the slightest storm comes into their life. Abundance will not enter your life as long as you are only thankful intermittently. Your gratitude must be steadfast and unmovable. In the Bible, Jonah called out "with a voice of thanksgiving" (Jonah 2:9) while in the belly of a great fish. We must have steady faith and believe that God's promises for our lives will work out for our good and His glory (Romans 8:28).

If we are consistent and faithful in being grateful while loving all, we can be inspired to do great things. Faith is about believing that God has not left us. If we believe, then we need to shout to the rooftops that God is great and His mercy endures forever.

Gratitude is a powerful, positive emotion/feeling. It creates powerful energy inside of us which is projected into the universe. We will never know all the mysteries of the universe. The energy which emanates from us is not fully understood but there are higher frequencies of energy centered on positive feelings. Paul explained in Ephesians 5:20: "Giving thanks always for all things to God the Father in the name of our Lord Jesus Christ."

I love the story of Job because it shows how being thankfully consistent leads us to a better life even under tragic circumstances. Adversity will come into everyone's life, this is a fact but it's how each of us deals with that adversity that will determine our destiny. After Job loses everything including his family, he states in Job 1:21, "Naked I came from my mother's womb, and naked shall I return there. The Lord gave and the Lord has taken away; Blessed be the name of the Lord." Further Job stated, "...Shall we indeed accept good from God, and shall we not accept adversity. In all this Job did not sin with his lips (Job 2:10)."

David stated in Psalm 26:7-8, "That I may proclaim with the voice of thanksgiving, and tell of all your wondrous works. Lord, I have loved the habitation of Your house, and the place where you glory dwells." There are many promises in the Bible but there are requirements levied on us to reap these promises. For example, Psalm 50 14-15 states, "Offer to God thanksgiving, and pay your vows to the Most High, Call upon Me in the day of trouble; I will deliver you, and you shall deliver glorify Me." In this verse, we are told to offer God thanksgiving first, and then we can call on the Lord to deliver us.

It's all an open secret that God has laid out a plan for us to have an abundant life and gratitude is part of that. Every day, I thank God for all the blessings He has given me over the years, and all the blessings that He was currently giving me and for all the gifts He will bestow on me in the future.

There is a section of the Bible written by Paul in Colossians 4:2-6 which is subtitled 'Christian Graces'. I found this section rich in great wisdom whether you are Christian or not. It says, "Continue earnestly in prayer, being vigilant in it with thanksgiving; meanwhile praying also for us, that God would open to us a door for the word, to speak the mystery of Christ, for which I am also in chains, that I may make it manifest, as I ought to speak. Walk in wisdom toward those who are outside, redeeming the time. Let your speech always be with grace, seasoned in salt, that you may know how you ought to answer each one." There is so much to comment on in this section--'being vigilant in prayer with thanksgiving' is an instruction for us to be steadfast in expressing our gratitude. Also we need to make the most out of each day by 'redeeming the time', the time wasted for pursuing the wrong things. I could write a whole book on that concept of redeeming the time but will save it for another time. The phrase that says, 'our speech always be with grace' means that we should speak what is spiritual, wholesome, fitting, kind, gentle, complimentary, truthful, loving and thoughtful. Speaking in this manner is an outward expression of our gratitude. God's credits and rewards will be appropriate to the attitude and action of our work. No good thing done for His glory will go unrewarded.

I often dance at night because I am thankful and want to be like David in the Bible as mentioned in the beginning, "And David dances with all of his might before the Lord (2 Samuel 6:14)." Dance danced for the Lord. God is great and has an amazing plan for our lives, being thankful shows that we trust God.

I close this section with a general thanksgiving from the Book of Common Prayer:

Almighty God, Father of all mercies, we, Your unworthy servants, give you humble thanks for all Your goodness and loving-kindness to us and to all men, We bless You for our creation, preservation, and all the blessings of this life; but above all for Your incomparable love in redemption of the world by our Lord Jesus Christ; for the means of grace, and for the hope of glory. And, we pray, give us such an awareness of Your mercies, that with truly thankful hearts we may make known Your praise, not only with our lips, but in our lives, by giving up ourselves to Your service, and by walking before You in holiness and righteousness all our days through Jesus Christ our Lord, to whom, with You and the Holy Spirit, be the honor and glory through the ages, Amen.

"Gratitude is not only the greatest of virtues, but the parent of all others."   Cicero

Chapter 17

Step Fifteen: *Read the Bible, spiritual devotionals and other great inspirational works daily.*

Each morning I look to fill my spiritual cup. A minister I knew once told me that if I overflow my internal spiritual cup on a daily basis, then it will ensure that there would be no space left for anything negative. When I decided to make a life change, I read as many religious books as I could each week. The more I gave God, the more I received each day. This step is about building spiritual muscle. Spiritual muscle provides inner nourishment for the soul and the spirit. When we feed both the spirit and the soul then we can rest and find joy. Reading the Bible, devotionals, or other great spiritual books provides guidance, wisdom, and promotes light into our lives.

My 20 steps were created to help me while I was in an internal negative place. The steps became new healthy habits in my life. Finding my spiritual core was not easy but it happened because I was open to reading great works and being open to a sincere spiritual path. It does not matter whether you follow my plan or someone else's. I have included two other plans at the end of this section; but to change, one must start following a new internal paradigm. Following a plan allows us to stay on purpose. Each of us must actively participate in our own rescue. We must actively participate in every moment of our lives by being fully engaged. Having a great appetite for life will allow us to grow and deal with the issues of our past.

"I found myself in myself." That said, I was guided by the Bible, and other great spiritual and inspirational books. At the end of this work is a list of books which helped me. Through the grace of God and the lessons I learned in those books, I decided that I did not want to live in "unhappiness" anymore. I was looking for God in all the wrong places. In the next step, I will discuss attending a house of worship; that step and this step are inter-related. We have to put God first in everything we do, not just on Sunday when we go to church but during the week. We need to view the world through a new paradigm, a clean and Godly heart. Sometimes God needs to knock us down to our knees to instruct us. In order to be instructed, I had to open my heart to a new way of doing things. I decided to focus on making lemonade with my perceived lemons everyday by doing something different--having a daily routine of studying every morning before I did anything else. My daily time with God allowed me to put Him first.

2 Corinthians 13:5 states, "Examine yourselves...test yourselves." Too few people actually examine themselves. I was one of those people who worked too hard and took little time for myself. I was living an unbalanced life and did not do anything to satisfy my soul.

Social psychology research indicated that at times of uncertainty, most people look to other people such as authority figures, peers, group norms, for their primary clues on how to proceed

(Robert B. Cialdini and Noah J. Goldstein, "Social Influence: Compliance and Conformity," Annual Review of Psychology, Feb 2004, 591-621). I decided to go on an inner quest when I became depressed years ago but I did not know where I was going. I just knew I had to move forward. The quest is a lonely one and you have to be brave enough to leave some things and people behind when you enter into a spiritually awakened state. Some people who are still living in the darkness will not understand and criticize or attempt to ridicule you but God wants you to move forward and lean into the light. The problem with the type of guidance from Cialdini and Goldstein above is that man is fallible, corruptible, and ultimately human. "The word of the Lord endures forever," as written in 1 Peter 1:25. We put too much value in what other defective humans think about us. We seek validation in everything we do, but it's God's validation we should be seeking. We need to have a close and personal relationship with God which can only come about by knowing God. We learn who God is through His word.

Before God can work through us, He must work on us. We must start a program to grow spiritually in order to nurture our relationship with Him. There is no better way to know God then spending time with Him, reading His word in the Bible, reflecting on what He has to say about how to live our life, and spending time in prayer. Reading His word in many different forms allow us to learn how to communicate with God more effectively. Keeping a daily appointment with God is an important part of living a true spiritual life. The more time we spend with God; by reading the Bible, praying, and meditating on His word, the closer our relationship becomes with Him. Once this happens, the more our lives will begin to reflect His image and His truth.

The value of the Bible consists not only in knowing it but obeying it. If we seek God's face, we will be rewarded beyond our imagination. We see things as we are, not as they really are. One eastern saying is: *If you are a hammer then everything you see looks like a nail.* We all need to retrain ourselves. I had to learn how to retrain myself by reading books and devotionals which fed my soul.

God is in you and God is in me--If we channel the light and the love--nothing will be withheld from us.

I did not live with enthusiasm before but after studying God's word, I realized that I had so much to be happy about. I realized who I was and whom I belonged to. The wisdom of how the seeker finds; can save your life as it did my life. I found great guidance and wisdom in the Bible and other spiritual books.

I started seeking to help myself by writing this book. I came to learn that when we help ourselves, we help the world. Leonard Griffith wrote, "*People are like prisoners, trapped in the dungeon of their own moral folly, the victims of evil rather than the doers of it. They started out with freedom of choice, but they continue to choose the wrong thing. The wrong choices become patterns of behavior that finally master those who made the choices.*" There are prisons of addiction to sex, drugs, alcohol, gambling, anger, sadness, and abuse. People are taken hostage by their own habits, behaviors, and conduct. The only way to break out of that rut is to make new healthier habits. To make a new habit, we must change our behavior. Some behaviors are called sticky because it's hard to get rid of. The new habits can be just as sticky but it will take retraining ourselves in new ways of doing things and handling issues in our lives.

How do you find your passion?By talking to God, and He will place it on your heart. In order to hear God, you need to draw closer to Him. We have to connect to our higher power. Make a plan each day to spend time with God even if its 15 minutes a day. Reading 'Our Daily Bread', 'the Upper Room', 'Days of Praise', 'The Word For You Today' or other devotional will increase the quality of your life and the likelihood of hearing God's voice.

Finding your passion; you must start a truth seeking journey. During the journey, open your mind along the way because everything that happens is a clue. All experiences point us in the right direction. Accept everything and everyone as a teacher along the way. I read Buddhist books, Hindu books, Sufi books, Gnostic books, Judaism books, Islamic mystic works, and hundreds of mainstream self-help books. Your truth seeking journey requires you to not judge. If you seek the truth aggressively, nothing will be withheld from you.

The Bible says in Philippians 2:12-13, "Work out your own salvation with fear and trembling; for it is God who works in you both to will and to do for His good pleasure."

The challenge before us is to see the world through eyes of Godly love. Jesus was trying to teach His disciples a new way to see the world and to live. Even though the disciples followed Jesus for almost three years, they still had doubt at times. We are the same but without Jesus to tell us directly, we have to rely on His word and teachings for guidance. I want to highlight an interesting point, while the faith of the disciples may have wavered at times, they didn't have all the revelation that we have in the form of the New Testament. We have all the instruction we need to live an abundant life.

It's never too late to change your life. It's never too late to attempt to find happiness. I know that many people have broken hearts, broken dreams, and broken promises in their past, but all of those experiences should be seen as your greatest teacher. Our goal in life is to acquire perfect balance. Too many people do not have balance because they are running through life at a chaotic pace. Their life is one of quiet and loud desperation, leading to the loss of balance. When you lose balance, you lose internal power. Being off balance leads to us having low negative energy in our daily lives.

Reading devotionals can open up new, exciting worlds which can inspire you to find your passion and purpose. I read a devotional called "At the feet of the Master" by Alcyone, published in 1984 by the Theosophical Publishing House. In this tiny 22 page book was great wisdom and a plan inside called the 'Six Points of Conduct' given by the Master:

1. Self-control as to the Mind: Controlling our desires, anger, or impatience and the mind itself. This is very much like my step 18 about how your thoughts can change your life. A calm mind draws courage which allows us to face trials on the path. Keep your mind from pride and never allow yourself to feel or depressed. Use your thought-power every day for good purposes. For example, each day think of someone in sorrow or suffering and send them loving thoughts.

2. Self-control in Action: If our thoughts are where they should be then we will have little trouble with our actions. If we are God's, then we must do ordinary work better than others. Do your own duty, not another person's. This is similar to my steps 1 and 6.

3. Tolerance: Feeling perfect tolerance for all. Free yourself from bigotry and open your heart. Tolerance to new beliefs and ideas. This is related to my steps 12 and step 3.

4. Cheerfulness: We must bear our karma cheerfully, whatever it may be. Cheerfulness also opens the heart. This is related to my steps 1 and 7.

5. One-pointedness: this means that nothing shall ever turn you, even for a moment, from the path upon which you have entered. Whatever you do, do it heartily, as to the Lord and not unto men. This is close to my step 19.

6. Confidence: Trusting God in all things. Trusting yourself by knowing who you are. This is close to my steps 9 and 17.

In another book I found published in 1954 by the late professor George G.M. James called Stolen Legacy. In that book, he wrote what he called the ten virtues for personal development:

1. Control of Thoughts.

2. Control of Actions.

3. Steadfastness

Every action a person engages in is a direct result of their thoughts; correct actions denote correct thought and steadfastness is the ability to maintain correct thoughts.

4. Identity with higher ideals.

5. Evidence of a mission

The ability to maintain correct thoughts and actions allows a person to experience the higher ideals that life has to offer.

6. Evidence of a call to spiritual order.

7. Freedom from resentment (courage)

Once people have experienced what they are missing in life, they are empowered by a call to spiritual order which in turn equips them with the necessary courage to face those still in darkness.

8. Confidence in the power of the master (teacher).

9. Confidence in one's own abilities.

10. Preparedness for initiation.

Every person who becomes properly motivated will encounter mentors and role models who will prepare them to assume positions of leadership. One must have confidence in the ability to exercise it correctly and prepare for the challenges awaiting them.

I find it interesting that many of the wisdom offered by others throughout history are similar. Reading spiritual works helps us to stay in the Spirit despite what's going on around us. We get what we aim at in every aspect of our lives; if we only put a few minutes during the week on spiritual matters or internal development then we will reap the benefits of that effort. There are parallel paths to salvation but we must stay teachable and open by reading new things. My reading list helped me to find and stay in the light.

Michelangelo stated at age 87, "*I am still learning.*"

"*The more you read, the more you know. The more you learn, the more places you go.*" Dr. Seuss.

Chapter 18

Step Sixteen: *Attend a house of worship weekly. Become a part of a spiritual community.*

My father once told me that the spiritual life needs to be made real. He said that we must 'make it real' which means that we must live it. Attending church or other house of worship helps us to make it real. Going to church weekly changed my life especially when I became a part of the community. After I started to see a change from going to church once a week, I started attending several services a week. I never understood the importance of going to church until I had nowhere else to turn, and then I figured it out. "I got it." I started developing my spiritual life and many other outlets opened in my life. I believe the difference in how "I got it" was that I had to 'make it real' by living it.

In the past, I just occasionally went to church and when nothing happened immediately, I rejected it as being worthless. We get out of life what we put into life. My breakthrough came as a result of developing my spiritual life. By cultivating my spirituality, a specific section inside of my soul became healed and fulfilled. The way to find that spiritual center is through attending a house of worship regularly. Regular attendance helps to teach you about that 'unique God shaped part' inside of each of our spirits that can only be filled and made whole by God.

Additionally, one must become a part of the community of believers and not just sitting in the seats and not becoming involved. Many people attend church each week and know no one there. I got so much out of singing the songs and praising God with other believers. I was able to prep my inner battlefield for the rest of the week by attending service and fellowshipping with others. I gained great insight about my faith from the sermons especially when I started to listen to my heart. I started attending Bible study classes and learned from others who attended.

Many who attend service each week do not engage with others, they just arrive and listen without becoming a part of the greater community. I started looking to hear God's voice during the sermon and through others at the church. I was always rewarded for my efforts. There were times when I was working on a chapter of this project and would be stuck. I would then go to church and God would literally put words on my heart to write about in that chapter or from the mouth of another believer in the Bible study class. We are on a pilgrimage for light and love, there are some routes which will take us to our destination. Attending a house of worship helps us to get to our destination.

"Blessed are those whose strength is in you, who have set their hearts on pilgrimage (Psalm 84:5)."

This step and step 15 is focused on growth. We were created to increase in life. When you stop learning, you stop growing. We have a responsibility to God to sharpen the skills we have and to develop new skills. Studies have shown that 50 percent of Americans do not read a whole book after finishing high school. If you invest in your spiritual development, you will be surprised at the ripple effect that will echo through all areas of your life. The people who develop their spiritual muscles get more blessings in life. Church should be viewed as a spiritual school and we should take our spiritual education seriously. Once I got into the church community, I started trading various inspirational books with others, and grew even more. Growth leads to living an inspired life! We are expected to continue to grow, not just continue to be static. If we work and are committed to making efforts to grow and move forward, God will bless us.

'Know Better' Life Principle: **God provides us more when we use the talents we have.**

Proverbs 18:16 states, "A man's gift makes room for him and brings him before great men." When we strive, God sees us and helps us to move in that same direction. Proverbs offers such great wisdom that I could quote numerous passages. I provide some of my favorite verse from Proverbs at the end of this book. I suggest that everyone read Proverbs regardless of their religious affiliation for wisdom.

'Know Better' Empowerment Exercise: Read one chapter of proverbs everyday for the next month (there are 31 chapters). Make notes of the verses that touch your heart. Write those verses down and keep them close, reading them often.

After reading Proverbs, start attending a good Bible based church, and you will be taken to a higher level. Proverbs 23:13 states, "Apply your heart to instruction, and your ears to words of knowledge."

Attending a house of worship regularly helps to apply your heart to instruction and prepare it for great spiritual blessings. Attendance helps one to become more spiritual. Spirituality involves the recognition and acceptance of a Higher Power beyond our own intelligence and willpower. I never had a real relationship with my Higher Power. In life, there are times when we do irresponsible things which reap unintended consequences. But there are times when we plan for success and reap the intended consequences of those actions. Attending church will reap intended consequences and positive side effects into your life. I discovered this fact and learned more about my Higher Power by working this step as well as steps 9, 10, and 15.

"...just as Christ also loved the church and gave Himself for her, that He might sanctify and cleanse her with the washing of water by the word, and that He might present her to Himself a glorious church, not having a spot or wrinkly or any such thing, but that she would be holy and without blemish (Ephesians 6:25-27)."

Spirituality and religion are two different things. Spirituality is the awareness of and the relationship with something greater than yourself and other human beings which exert control over all aspects of our lives. Spirituality is a respect for that All-Mighty Power or force in the universe. If we cultivate our religious life, then other areas of our lives will improve. I do not know if it was a miracle from God or just working my steps which helped me to rise out of the abyss I was in. Many people like to explain why they can't go to church, "Look at those hypocrites attending church (Are you going to church for their salvation or your salvation)" or "I prefer to worship alone (but in reality you don't)", or "I'm not religious, I'm spiritual (What does that really mean when you really don't have a robust spiritual practice)", or my favorite, "I don't have time (but you have time for everything else)." It would be a shame if when you called on God, God would tell you He did not have the time to listen. I want to provide reasons why I go to a house of worship as much as possible, not just one day a week.

--Praise and worship: First and foremost, I make an effort and outward expression to God by singing and praising Him in His house of Worship. I can do this at home, but in my faith (Christianity) it says that when two or more are gathered, God is in the midst. I am able to sing and praise Him in a fashion more worthy of who He is. We are called to serve God. We can serve Him anywhere but places of worship allow for the service to be focused. It's about God; too many people look around when they should be looking up.

--Safety and Security: We all have anxieties, stresses, worries, fears, and perhaps panic attacks. All of these issues come from a variety of reasons: heredity, biology, family background, conditioning, your self-talk, personal belief system, your ability to express yourself, past traumas, and/or abuse. Regardless of the reasons, you will find comfort and security in attending a house of worship. In that place, you will learn how to rely on and develop a relationship with your Higher Power. You gain security through the conviction that you are not alone in the world as you worship with others. You will learn that there is no problem too great or difficult for God. Also, if you are in trouble, there is no better place to go for answers than a place of worship. It's a safe haven from the chaos of the world.

--Inner Peace: This is a result from feeling a deep and profound sense of safety and security. As you grow and trust your Higher Power, it will become easier to deal with life without worry or anxiety. For me, being in church and singing to God gave me much inner peace. I felt loved and accepted in church. Peace came to me through letting go while in church. If we attend a house of worship giving ourselves up to God then we will start to understand the peace which surpasses all understanding. After attending church for several years, when I walked into church, I would start to feel more peaceful. I had reprogrammed myself to see Sundays as God's day. I received the best therapy I ever had by attending church and listening with an open heart and mind.

--Understanding the Love: I never even understood the concept of love until I started attending church and hearing other Christian brothers say they loved me. Love me? How could anyone love me? I learned how God loved me and I saw fellow believers express their love for me. I started to experience greater degrees of understanding unconditional love through my attendance. I felt a loving sense within the community and through the church. I started opening my heart to strangers and felt more love for all. My heart learned about unconditional love and how to love others in the same way. In my religion, I trusted and opened my heart and received love in return. The bible says in Matthew 6:33, "First seek the Kingdom of heaven and all will be added unto you." The start of my journey to seek the Kingdom was through being a part of a good-bible based church.

--Guidance: I gained guidance in how to make God-conscious decisions from the Word and the elders in the church. I was able to increase my level of understanding on all things spiritual. God provided me with much wisdom while in church listening to a sermon or hearing a hymn. I would be thinking about a concept like forgiveness and then the minister would start preaching on that same topic. Further, God would start to place specific scriptures on my heart that I could not remember before. I started to develop flashes of intuition through my spiritual practice and from being in the house of the Lord. My intuitive flashes became very accurate. I learned how to pray through watching elders in the church and I learned what to pray for. I had never even expressed in a prayer to God the following, "I love you God!" before I started my journey in church. Church became my new school and place of learning where I gained Christian values. My growth came in part because of my attendance I use my experience in the church but I encourage everyone to develop their spirituality by attending a house of worship.

--Getting to know God through His house of worship: God became more real when I started going to church. Inspiration and intuition can come in many forms including just sitting in a house of worship meditating on His word. Our prayer life can be magnified when we do it with others in a church or another place or worship. "Praising God and having favor with all people. And the Lord added to the church daily those who were being saved (Acts 2:47)." The church (or house of worship) should be the center of our lives because out of those walls emits strong spiritual blessings and energy.

We have more options and technology than our parents ever had but we are less happy. I think it's because of a spiritual void inside of us. Less people today attend houses of worship than in our parent's generation. Also, I think too few people have not found their unique purpose in life. Each of us has one or more special purposes to fulfill which gives our life a sense of meaning and completeness. Those people who fully realize their special purpose in life feel more satisfied and often live longer, happier lives. Finding and fulfilling our life purpose has a two-fold benefit: 1) We feel more complete and whole thus bringing more light into the world vice adding more chaos; and 2) A beneficial impact on all those around us.

Everyone likes to keep their options open in society today. Some options should not be open, like how to live an upright life. God wants us to be committed. Options create shallow believers. We are already fully equipped and don't need options for worship. What does God want for our life? This step may focus on attendance at the Lord's House but it's bigger than that. Making a weekly or twice weekly effort to worship God in his house is a sign of our faithfulness and commitment to Him.

Igniting that fire within comes when we love the things that God loves. Attendance in God's house should not be an option. Excuses will not lead to salvation, but seeking God's face will.

Being with fellow believers also helps one get "in the Spirit." The Bible says that God will be in the midst when 2 or more are gathered in His name. Never underestimate the power of prayer in a group of like-minded individuals to create miracles.

Make your spiritual practice real, and inner happiness will be yours.

Chapter 19

Step Seventeen: *Have faith! Faith and fear both require that we believe in something we cannot see. Faith and fear are opposite muscle groups and cannot be flexed at the same time. Believe that you can change and work ambitiously towards that goal, and it will happen.*

Jesus says in Mark 5:36, "...Do not be afraid; only believe."

Mark 9:23 states, "Jesus said to him, 'If you can believe, all things are possible to him who believes.

The above quotes are about belief and faith. Faith should be expressed 24 hours a day. Our goal should center on strengthening our spiritual natures so that we are steadfast and consistent in our faith. We should strive to have faith in God, in ourselves and in the process. Having faith and trusting the process that God has started in you will allow you to have more inner joy because you are no longer worrying about the past or the future.

"Whoever ... does not doubt in his heart, but believes that those things he says will be done, he will have whatever he says (Mark 11:23)." This is the blessing of the prayer of faith of which Jesus speaks. Believe that you have already received and trust in God each day. The world is one of infinite possibilities, and faith creates balance.

My 20 steps of empowerment and love were born out of a desire to help myself become whole and healthy. I met with various religious leaders, priests, clerics, ministers, mystics, holy men and shaman over the years to gain more perspective on life. I was inspired after God put it on my heart that there was a better way. I took everything I learned and decided to make a more specific guide for myself and I hope that this work helps your too. I want to show others how to tap into that inner power.

"The steadfast love of the Lord never ceases, his mercies never come to an end; they are new every morning; great is your faithfulness (Lamentations 3:22)."

As adults, many of us do not naturally trust, believe and have faith in God. Thus we need to build our faith through working a system of steps centered on reading God's word. We tend to drift in and out of living by faith. The Bible states in Romans 10:17, "So then faith comes by hearing, and hearing by the word of God." By focusing on increasing our faith by reading the word of God, we are reprogramming ourselves. Reading the Bible and/or other spiritual/inspirational great works, along with prayer, allows one's faith to increase. Many people only pray when things are bad and they are looking for something from God.

"*I would rather err on the side of faith than on the side of doubt.*" Pastor Robert Schuller

In Romans, Paul writes about faith in 10:8-11, "...The word is near you, in your mouth and in your heart (that is, the word of faith which we preach); that if you confess with your mouth the Lord Jesus and believe in your heart that God has raised Him from the dead, you will be saved. For with the heart one believes unto righteousness, and with the mouth confession is made, unto salvation. For the Scripture says, Whosoever believes on Him will not be put to shame."

In Buddhism, there is a concept called the Buddha nature. The Buddha nature means that the seed of mindfulness and enlightenment is in every person, representing our potential to become fully awake. There is true wisdom in the Buddhist's path because they offer parallel beliefs which help us move towards a spiritual awakening. Faith can move mountains and fear can tear them down. If we train our mind to be disciplined then we will not go into the bad neighborhoods of the mind so often until we no longer go into them at all.

A woman who had the flow of blood for 12 years sought out Jesus because she had faith as described in Luke 8:48. She was healed when she touched Jesus' garment. Jesus says to her, "Daughter, be of good cheer, your faith has made you well. Go in peace." We can all have good cheer and inner joy if we cast our cares on God. All we need to do is to believe. In Mathew 17:20, we learn that the disciplines of Jesus could not cure a man suffering severely. The disciples asked why they could not cast the demon out of the man. Jesus said to them, "Because of your unbelief; for assuredly, I say to you, if you have faith as a mustard seed, you will say to this mountain; Move from here to there, and it will move; nothing will be impossible for you."

Jesus explained that faith was key, "Knowing that a man is not justified by the works of the law but by faith in Jesus Christ, even we have believed in Christ Jesus that we might be justified by faith in Christ and not by the works of the law; for by the works of the law no flesh shall be justified (Galatians 2:16)." Faith always triumphs in trouble. Faith can channel the inner fire inside of us. God is within us and that fire is stoked by our faith.

Channel away all negative energy and focus on love in order to achieve whatever you set your mind on for the next five minutes. This is a meditative exercise to visualize the type of life you want. Focus on what you want to draw into your life. Do this daily.

"Therefore, having been justified by faith, we have peace with God through our Lord Jesus Christ, through whom also we have access by faith into this grace in which we stand, and rejoice in the hope of the glory of the Lord (Romans 5:1-2)."

The 11th chapter of Hebrews describes faith. In the first verse, "Now faith is the substance of things hoped for, the evidence of things not seen." In the third verse of the chapter, "By faith, we understand that the worlds were framed by the word of God, so that the things which are seen were not made of things which are visible." Faith pleases God. True faith is not based on empirical evidence but on divine assurance, and is a gift of God (Ephesians 2:8). True saving faith works with obedience to God.

2 Corinthians 5:7 states, "For we walk by faith, not by sight." The Christian can hope for a heaven he has not seen. He does so by believing what the Bible says about it and living by that belief. Faith is about believing and trusting in God. Once we are able to burn off those negative, ungodly thoughts and behaviors, it's easier to hear God's voice on a daily basis. Isaiah 30:21 states, "Your ears shall hear a word behind you saying, 'This is the way, walk in it,' Whenever you turn to the right hand of whenever you turn to the left." Once we change our thinking and our actions, God's voice will be there for us to hear.

Later in Isaiah 40:31 we learn, "But those who wait on the Lord shall renew their strength; they shall mount up with wings like eagles, they shall run and not be weary, they shall walk and not be faint." Trusting in God gives us amazing power!

I read a poem from David Jeremiah's book 'When you World Falls Apart' which I found very powerful regarding faith:

> *Sometimes we come to life's crossroads,*
> *And we view what we think is the end.*
> *But God has a much wider vision,*
> *And He knows that it's only a bend--*
> *The road will go on and get smoother,*
> *and After we've stopped for a rest,*
> *The path that lies hidden beyond us,*
> *Is often the path that is best.*
> *So rest and relax and grow stronger,*
> *Let go and let God share your load,*
> *And have faith in a brighter tomorrow.*
> *You've just come to a bend in the road.*

'Know Better' Life Principle: **Living worry free in the present moment, demonstrates our faith in God.**

Faith is demonstrated when we make the present moment, our friend. When we accept the present, and don't judge it, we can live fully in that instant. Most problems are man-made, created in our mind. We don't really have trust in God, which is why we worry. We fall short in how we show our faith in God. We pray repeatedly for the same thing every night. If we trust in God, then we should give it to God and trust God to work it out. After you pray and give it to God, live life expectantly.

Your life is now. Pay close attention and enjoy your life as it unfolds without the anxiety, worry or stress. If we believe and trust in God, then we can live in the present moment worry-free. Having faith and believing allows us to live in the "Now". We can enjoy life, living in the moment because we are trusting God to do His job. We all have a job to do, serve God and do what is pleasing in God's eyes. We can all relax today because God is in charge and does not need our help. "Give your entire attention to what God is doing right now, and don't get worked up about what may or may not happen tomorrow. God will help you deal with whatever hard things come up when the time comes (Mathew 6:34)."

Living confidently in the moment is based on not worrying about the past or stressed out about the future. Living in the "now" or present helps us to stay focused on what is important. Once we start being more mindful, then our lives become more manageable and joyful. The Buddha stated, "How wonderful! How wonderful! All things are perfect exactly as they are!" When the Buddha (the enlightened or awakened one) realized perfect enlightenment, the veils of the worldly illusions feel away. Living in the present moment was one of his goals. If we attend to the present moment then all of life's positive energies will have the opportunity to meet: motivation, intention, aspiration, hope and expectation. The present moment is where we can engage our body, mind and spirit.

Self-awareness leads to self-transformation. Awareness is curative. Buddhism provided me with great wisdom which I could integrate into my spiritual practice. Mindfulness helps us to live in the present and to awaken. This part of the step is based on having present moment awareness. We need to liberate ourselves by fully trusting God. God has given us all we need. Jesus stated, "The kingdom of God is within you (Luke 17:21)." We have all the power we will ever need already inside of us. If we can fully trust and have faith in God, we can tap into the creative power already inside of us. To tap into that power, we must get out of our way mentally by not judging everything. Just be and have faith in God, the transformative process will start.

Faith equals power.

If you can eradicate your unbelief while maintaining pure and honest intentions, unlimited power will be yours.

By practicing mindfulness each day, you will be able to develop your inner power. Start by simply being present and fully aware without judging or any negative bias. Use mindfulness to just be in the "now". Take a deep breath and completely relax. Focus on breathing deeply into and out of the diaphragm. Count each breath until you get to 10 and then count back down to 1. For example: Inhale, count one to yourself. Exhale, count two to yourself. Inhale count three to yourself. Exhale, count four to yourself. Continue this until 10. Be completely in the present, the only moment that matters, is this moment. Be present, awake and aware of your body. With each breath, let go of fear, anger, anxiety, regret, cravings, frustration. Embrace love, forgiveness for others and yourself. Let go of the need for approval. Feel God's love. Focus on accepting yourself and others. Center your breathing on love. Do this exercise daily and it will allow you to stay in the present moment while moving you towards transformation.

The Buddha explained an eight-fold path for enlightenment:

1) Right View

2) Right Intention

3) Right Speech

4) Right Action

5) Right Livelihood

6) Right Effort

7) Right Mindfulness

8) Right Concentration

The living Buddha, the sixteenth Karmapa stated, "*If you have one hundred percent dedication and confidence in Dharma (purpose) teachings, every living situation can be part of a spiritual practice.*" Buddhist Lama Yeshe provides the below practices as a way to bring inner peace into your life every day thus allowing you to be present and stay faithful to the transformation process:

Pray

Meditate

Be Aware / Stay Awake

Bow

Practice Yoga

Chant

Feel

Chant and Sing

Breath and Smile

Relax / Enjoy / Laugh / Play

Create / Envision

Let go / Forgive / Accept

Walk / Exercise / Move

Work / Serve / Contribute

Listen / Learn / Inquire

Consider / Reflect

Cultivate Oneself / Enhance competencies

Cultivate Contentment

Cultivate Flexibility

Cultivate Friendship and Collaboration

Open up / Expand / Include

Lighten up

Dream

Celebrate and Appreciate

Give Thanks

Evolve

Love

Share / Give / Receive

Walk Softly / Live gently

Expand / Radiate / Dissolve

Simplify

Surrender / Trust

Be Born Anew

1 Corinthians 16:13 states, "Watch, stand fast in the faith, be brave, be strong. Let all that you do be done with love." Faith creates the conditions for a beautiful and abundant life. I had been seeking for many years but could never slow down to find it. I didn't even know what I was looking for. God helped me to slow down and look within. Looking within, I learned how to fill that unique God-shaped place in my soul. As stated above Jesus said, 'the kingdom of God was within' but I just did not know where to look before.

"Faith is seeing light with your heart when all your eyes see is darkness." Anonymous

"God didn't promise days without pain, laughter without sorrow, or sun without rain, but He did promise strength for the day, comfort for the tears, and light for the way. If God brings you to it, He will bring you through it." Unknown

"The antidote to frustration is a calm faith, not in your own cleverness, or in hard toil, but in God's guidance." Norman Vincent Peale

Chapter 20

Step Eighteen: *Think pure and good thoughts. Always have honest intentions. You can change your life by changing your thinking.*

I believe that anyone reading this work can achieve greatness, happiness and success in any endeavor they pursue. This can only happen if they master their thoughts. We are the master of our thoughts and character. We are the maker and shaper of our own lives and fate. Our minds were made for good because good is the basic elemental forces of the universe.

I think the difference between people who are successful in life and those who aren't is based on finding one's purpose and meaning in life. The people who can get out of their mental way, moving beyond the past conditioning in order to live the grand life God intended them, go on to paint that amazing work of art or write that super symphony or pen that best seller.

I believe the difference is based on how people think. I put forward that anyone can maximize their potential and ignite that fire within if one has an operational life plan. You are meant to have an amazing life. You are meant to have everything you love. You are your thoughts. Proverbs 23:7 states that, "So as a man is in his heart, so is he."

The revolution will not be televised; because the revolution will be in our mind. I believe that there is a drive inside of us, to better ourselves. Throughout history, there have been individuals who have been able to solve near impossible problems or risen to higher levels of creativity. Some people have been able to gain inspiration and insight much higher than the rest of their contemporaries. I have always been amazed at the people able to have intense inner clarity. I have studied great men in the hopes that I could learn from them. I never had a serious spiritual component in my life before. So, I decided to turn my will over to God and was only able to transform my life by changing the way I thought. Many people want to change.

'Know Better' Life Question: Why is change so difficult?

I think it's because of our thinking, our defective thinking. A person is literally what they think, their character being the entire sum of their thoughts. We shape our own destinies whether we know it or not. The great spiritual traditions all agree that in our untrained state of mind; awareness, insight and perception are impaired by our shaky emotional states, our distorted views of reality and our uncontrollable desires. I have always believed that one is either in control, under control or out of control.

It has been said many times that, "we do not see things are they are but as we are."

We make new year resolutions but usually quit after a few days or weeks. Why is that? In 2010, Americans spent 11 billion dollars on self improvement products and services. The excellent book written by Rick Warren of Saddleback Church called *The Purpose Driven Life* sold approx

40 million copies. Stephen Covey's *The Seven Habits of Highly Effective People* sold 20 million copies. We all struggle with purpose and meaning. Maybe there is something inside of us which propels us forward to be better but why do some people have no trouble turning it around while others struggle their whole life for balance and inner peace. I want to add that 50 million people in the United States are on anti-depressants. That is about 1 out of every six Americans. Why are we so unhappy and unfulfilled as a species? What are we so depressed?

The Buddhists text, *the Dhammapada*, verse 1-2 state, *"All that we are is the result of what we have thought. All that we are is founded on our thoughts and formed of our thoughts. If a man speaks or acts with an evil thought, pain pursues him as a wheel of a wagon follows the hoof of the ox that pulls it. If a man speaks or acts with a pure thought, happiness pursues him like his own shadow that never leaves him."*

For better or worse, the thoughts that we plant in our mind will eventually manifest in our lives. Jesus said in Mark 9:23, "Everything is possible for the person who believes."

Romans 12:2 explains, "Be not conformed to this world but be ye transformed by the renewing of your mind, that you may prove what is good, and acceptable, and the perfect will of God."

You mind works perfectly--it works the way that it was programmed or conditioned, until you reprogram it. Most people live in the prisons of their own making. Constantly being swayed by the whims of the worlds, getting upset, stressed out by the waves of life.

Jim Rohn explained, *"Your life does not get better by chance, it gets better by change."*

The key to transforming one's life is to take advantage of that tragedy life had thrown us to realign our lives along spiritual lines. We all have mental housekeeping to do. Staying in the good neighborhoods of the mind is very important. We can all dwell on the past and take offense to what everyone says about us but why bring suffering into your life. Too many people fight the wrong battles in their mind. They transfer their bad feelings onto other people. They do not know themselves well enough to gauge where the pain is coming from. I mentioned earlier about controlling the inner dialogue and this step is a part of that. It starts with controlling the inner dialogue and then creating the conditions necessary for success. The condition for success is all about right thinking. Thinking noble, good, honest and Godlike thoughts is right thinking. Right thinking achieves positive results.

An Eastern mystic once told me, *"It is most possible for you, while you are inside a cage, to look out upon the horizon and to smell the roses. It is also extremely possible for you to be in a castle full of opulence and comfort, and yet be angry and discontented with your family and wealth."* I now understand that phrase because it is all in how one sees it in their mind. I had what some would call "having it all" but I was so unhappy and I did not understand that I had the power within to change. I always needed something on the exterior to make me happy.

How do you master your thoughts? We can master our thoughts through triage just like in battle. In combat, when someone is injured, medics do triage to administer immediate medical care.It's a battle within our mind. Just like in battle, we need to do triage when we are injured. We have been conditioned and that conditioning is like an injury. As such, we need to do triage of our thoughts. In battle, you examine the injury and then stabilize the vitals before you administer the treatment so you can move the victim to a better medical facility. My plan for mental triage is:

First: Examine your thoughts. Start a daily thought log for 21 days to get a handle on how you think. The mind is like a dog running wild without a leash. The mind has also been compared to a monkey chasing a shiny object. Identify the underlying patterns in order to position yourself to change it. Put virtuous thoughts in your mind. Steadfastly maintain these thoughts: love, joy, peace, forgiveness, compassion, goodness, gentleness, hope, serenity, long-suffering and kindness. Remove any thoughts of vice such as foul language, anger, fault-finding, judging, strife, sexual immorality, lust, greed, pride, ego (which means easing God out), envy, jealousy, stealing, lying ect. This is where you will have to fight, fight for your victory. If you elevate your thoughts, the circumstances in your life will elevate too.

Second: Stabilize your thoughts by stopping during the day and taking you mental temperature. Start to take moments throughout the day to monitor your thoughts realizing what your underlying beliefs are and what needs to be replaced. Meditation and prayer can help in this step. We focus on what we will eat or watch on TV; use this step to concentrate on what you are thinking about. Do not judge what you are thinking; just change your inner dialogue. Prayer can help in this step.

Third: Administer treatment by changing that inner dialogue or mental housekeeping as I call it. You can change the inner dialogue by reading spiritual literature and filling your internal spirit with good things each day. Start to think about all those people you have grudges against and begin to pray for them. Start to bless your enemies, do it for yourself in order to change your life. You need to understand that your true self-worth is based being a child of the most high God. God is the best treatment in the world. Believing that He can and will change you is the best medicine. You must see the change already in your mind's eye. Replace wrong thinking with right thinking by working the other steps of attending a house of worship, exercising, forgiving, loving, helping, ect. Every day, do one specific activity for your mental health. Choose new routines and patterns for your life while rejecting the old patterns. Let your mind be still or quiet several times a day, every day, through mindful meditation.

First of all, you will have more inner peace and serenity if you quiet your mind by just 20 percent. You can achieve this effect of quieting the mind but first you must monitor your thoughts to see what you are doing. Most people do not even realize what they do unconsciously throughout the day. Watching your thoughts and then changing them can change your life.

This is all about you, your recovery and healing to become more whole and healthy. Stop letting others control your mind by how they feel or what they think about you.

William James stated, "*Most people live, whether physically, intellectually or morally, in a very restricted circle of their potential being. They make use of a very small portion of their possible consciousness...We all have reservoirs of life to draw upon, of which we do not dream.*"

We need to understand and become more aware of the unlimited power we have to create our future. We each have within us the transformative power inside to change our lives. In the ancient Hindu text of Bhagavad Gita in the 5th century BC, we learn that, "*the mind acts like an enemy for those who do not control it.*" We are prisoners of our own mind. Sigmund Freud stated that, "*man is not even master in his own house... his own mind.*" Free yourself this day!

'Know Better' Life Principle: **The 'Law of Conditionality' states that most often, we have the conditions for our own happiness already. Happiness occurs by living in the present moment.**

The Buddha provided four noble truths: 1) to exist is to suffer; 2) Suffering comes from desires or cravings; 3) Suffering will end when we removes their cravings or desires; 4) We can strip off the delusions of the world and see the world as it is through the eight-fold path for enlightenment (this is mentioned earlier). I provide this as further insight to help you transform. I came up with my own truths:

> *1--You have the power to change the way you think. Own yourself.*

> *2--You have been conditioned and programmed. Our parents did the best they could but many of them came from dysfunctional families too. Deal with the past and generational curses so that others will not have to. It's your responsibility to be better. Serving God will allow you to live up to your potential. If you had Typhoid, you would not go outside spreading the disease. Well, we are all broken on the inside from the past, start to deal with the past in positive, constructive ways. Stop reliving the painful events of the past. Integrate those experiences in a positive healthy way into your life. Stop fighting the wrong battles in your mind.*

> *3--Change your life by changing your thinking. The goal is to master you mind by observing your thoughts. Prep the battlefield for success through right thinking. Right thinking will allow you to make the universe work for you. If you dwell on negative thoughts then you will achieve negative results. Positive thoughts achieve positive results. Stop focusing on how others make you feel. All humans are as beautiful and as loved as they believe they are. Good thoughts bare good fruit.*

George Eliot stated, "*It's never too late to be who you might have been.*"

'Know Better' Tools of Success

Love, kindness, understanding, forgiveness, compassion, generosity, faith, self-control, making goals, purity, hope, prayer and meditation.

Tools of failure

Foul language, anger, hate, unforgiveness, wrath, envy, greed, jealousy, doubt, selfishness and drift

The devil loves to drop seeds of doubt and negativity in your minds. The devil loves to make your think bad thoughts or think less of yourself. The biggest lie of the devil is that you cannot change, that you are stuck in the same circumstance forever.

You are a child of the King, the Most High God! You were made in the image of God, align your thoughts to that of God and you will become unconquerable. The power is inside of you. Right now, most people's thoughts are filled with such doubt and negativity that their conscious mind do not even detect that negative self-talk anymore. Get your mind on a leash, and your hand firmly on the leash.

When I gave my life to Christ, I began to see God directing my path and His hand in my daily activities. God wants us to choose live and to thrive. Each crisis is an opportunity to dig deeper, find our spiritual center, and learn about God so we can become stronger and more balanced. We can choose to not allow any situation make us more negative and unbalanced. We can choose the light. We choose to not let our circumstances affect our attitude.

Always remember that '**happiness is a choice'.**

Chapter 21

Step Nineteen: *Do everything with a passion. Live with an inner fire. Live your passions daily. Passion equals power!*

Too few people actually live their passions. Proverbs says, "Hope defers makes a heart sick." Living our dreams will heal those past hurts. There are many people out here who has allowed the devil to steal their dreams. The devil is real and has many people working on his team. The devil's agents are ready to steal your dream and take your inner joy. Happy people live longer and are more productive according to scientists. Living with passion helps us to live a life of meaning.

Get excited about life! Love yourself, love your day and love your life!

God gave you this life and wants you to be happy, whole and healthy. No matter what is going in your life, get excited because God loves you and is for you. Every day you have a reason to get up. Draw on the power in the universe and from God; know that you are not alone. God is with you. I decided to help myself because I knew God has already done His part-He gave me all I needed to help myself.

The devil will do anything to discourage you and keep you from being the person God intended you to be. The devil wants you to be depressed and he puts negative thoughts in your head telling you that you can't live your dreams, it's only going to fail. But the devil is a liar. I am here to tell you that God wants you to live passionately with an inner fire.

2 Timothy 1:6, states, "Therefore I remind you to stir up the gift of God which is in you through the laying on of my hands. For God has not given us a spirit of fear, but of power and of love and of a sound mind." God has given us the power, we must passionately use the gifts that God has given us to the fullest. We need to be stirred up on the inside. We must continue to keep that fire stirred up by working a plan. These steps are a part of my plan to keep my passion stirred up. When life tries to beat you down, you must tap into that God given power to stir yourself up. You are not alone, God is with you and the Holy Spirit will empower you to do more than you could do on your own.

God is amazingly wonderful! In James 4:8, "If you draw near to God, then God will draw near to you". In Islam, there is the same guidance, 'take one step towards Allah and He will take one step towards you.' Have a passion and live your passions -- God is pleased when we live a rich life.

There are unfortunate people out here who are still living in darkness while others have found the light and are trying to recover. Once you are on the path to being healed, now what? This is the stage of discovery. Discover your passion, if you don't already know what it is then it's time to stretch those muscles that you have not used previously. Discovering your God given mission in life will inspire you to create great works. What were you meant to be, not your job but what great things were you meant to do or create?

Too many people are stuck in the past. After you move beyond that past pain, hurt and disappointment, it's time to move forward to a place where God will put your talents to work. We are becoming more defective than our parent's generation. We now have defective people raising future defective kids. We are over-medicated and under-loved. There too many broken homes, addictions, cycles of abuse, violence and crime than ever before.

Romans 12:6 states, "We have different gifts, according to the grace give us." We each have gifts which some of us have not even discovered. We will all continue to be spiritually sick if we are not living the life God intended us to live. We will stay sick on the inside if we are not using our talents in the right areas and doing what we were meant to do.

Life is meant to be easy, not a daily struggle. Too many people voluntarily live in "bad neighborhoods of their mind." Most people are so engaged in many negative activities that they never think about inner happiness. The bad neighborhood sets people up for failure. We must always stay teachable. Too many people are intransigent and resistant to change. We should look passionately for the lesson is every situation. The devil wants you to be unteachable and unchangeable.

I wanted to provide some suggestions on how to ignite that fire inside, a framework for success.

1-Understand the internal conditions of your life; past habits and routines. By understanding your past, you can escape the old patterns.

2-Identify an objective or goal having to do with your untapped passion.

3-Make a plan to reach the goal regarding your passion--a brand new plan. Brainstorm and ask others about their passions in get ideas about your passion.

4-Execute the necessary steps of this new plan at least on a weekly basis.

5-Stay focused and don't let anyone take you off your path. Continue to adjust to the new paradigm where people may try to dissuade you from your passion.

We all have our share of good or bad habits. These steps are focused on moving beyond the old habits and replacing them with new, more positive habits. We were meant to not only survive but to thrive. The Apostle Paul stated, "Therefore He says: Awake, you who sleep, Arise from the dead, and Christ will give you light (Ephesians 5:14)!" We have to get excited and revved up about life. All of my steps work together with one another. If you put them all together then you will have the power to change your life from the inside.

People need to make a conscious decision to live the life that they were meant to live. The human capacity to derail themselves is amazing but we also have the power to put the train back on the rails to reach our destination. Life can be so rich and meaningful but it will take effort on our part. I want to empower people to realize that they determine the outcome of their lives. Live your dream! Get you fire back and keep the flames stocked inside of you.

In Iran, there was an old called Zoroastrism and their main concept is having good thoughts, words and deeds. There are still some Zoroastrians out here today. The Zoroastrians lived mainly in the 9th or 10th century BC. Their key beliefs centered on a transcendent creator, God called Ahura Mazda, and the concept of free will. They viewed the world as dualist with an adversary called Ahriman. In their worldview, they believed that one could prevent chaos if one chose to serve God and exercised good thoughts, works and deeds. Their religious book the Avesta stated, "*Taking the first footstep with a good thought, the second with a good word, and the third with a good deed, I entered Paradise.*" They had a revenant view of fire, some called them fire worshippers. We can all enter Paradise here on earth by embracing change through our individual actions. Once we decide to do something different and execute the steps for that change, the fire inside of us will be ignited. I think discussing the Zoroaster is so appropriate because I want to help others ignite that fire inside which will help to bring about inner happiness. I brought up this ancient religion to show that throughout history there has been great wisdom repeated throughout time.

William Carey was an ordinary man who went on to do great things as a missionary in the 18th century. He had extraordinary faith, reading much theology and many journals of explorers. Through his study, he became interested in the world and eventually went to India to spread God's word as an evangelist. He learned Indian dialects into which he translated the Bible. Carey was a shoemaker but went to do great things. His passion for his missions is expressed in his own words, "*Expect great things from God; attempt great things for God.*" He lived out this philosophy and thousands were led to do missionary work because of his example.

The Bible tells us of the great faith of many people who went on to do great things. In Hebrews it says, "who through faith subdued kingdoms, worked righteousness, obtained promises, stopped the mouths of lions, quenched the violence of fire, escaped the edge of the sword, out of weakness were made strong (Hebrews 11:33)." Because of God's power and faithfulness, we can do all things through Christ who strengthens us (Philippians 4:13).

'Know Better' Life Principle: **Expect great things from God; attempt great things for God each day.**

If we get excited about life and our passions then we can go on to do great things in life. Work towards living your passion today. Do one thing that you have never done but wanted to do such as start painting, writing, composing, working out, starting that business plan, or volunteering. It called life because it's meant to be lived!

Wake up each morning and tell yourself, "God is with me and wants me to thrive today." You have the power inside to affect your outer circumstances. You don't have to be a victim to your random thoughts.

One time during my search for knowledge, I went to a gathering of Mata Amritanandamayi, an Indian guru known as Amma or mother. She is best known for literally embracing millions of people around the world. She has hugged millions of people including myself one day on tour in America. I saw throngs of people lingering inside the back room of the hotel waiting to be hugged by Amma. She has earned the nickname of the "hugging saint". I waited in line for about an hour before I received my hug. During the hugging, she whispered in my ear. I felt a wave of love and affection that I had not felt before. As I was leaving, I felt a strong, positive energy over my life and was given a Hershey's chocolate kiss by one of her assistants before I left. I will always remember Amma's passion. I learned from her assistants that she travels the world giving hugs. Her devotees in India view her as a demi-god and say she has performed miracles such as diverting storms. Her status as a spiritual therapist has attracted a large following in the United States. Amma may be in her late 50's now but she seemed to have unlimited energy because of her passion for what she does. I read in an interview that she said, "I am connected to the eternal energy source, so I am not like a battery that gets used up." Amma has established a vast organization to help others; from nothing, she has built a charitable empire. During the Tsunami devastating India in 2004, she built more than 600 houses. Her global charitable organization helps thousands each year.

If we strive to do great things in the name of love, nothing will be withheld from us. The peace I was looking for was inside all the time. We need to make every minute count by getting fired up about life!

'Know Better' Life Principle: **Get passionate about God and He will get passionate about you!**

This step goes into the next step because passion leads to "praying big, loving big and hoping big" and doing all three boldly!!

Hebrew 12:29 states, "For our God is a consuming fire." The fire is already in us, because as John says in 4:6, "We are of God."

Steve Jobs said, *"Your time is limited, so don't waste it living someone else's life. Don't be trapped by dogma – which is living with the results of other people's thinking. Don't let the noise of others opinions drown out your own inner voice. And most importantly, have the courage to follow your heart and intuition. They somehow already know what you truly want to become. Everything else is secondary."*

Chapter 22

Step 20 - <u>Pray Big, Love Big and Hope Big</u>

Within these three simple concepts everything else falls easily into place. God wants so much for us. It's in His word. Read the scriptures of the Christian faith. God has given us the guide to live an amazing life.

'Know Better' Life Principle: **<u>Pray Big, Love Big and Hope Big!</u>** These three 'Know Better' Life Principles can transform your life because within each principle are the seeds of victory.

Within prayer is belief and faith. Meditation is part of prayer.

Within Love there is forgiveness, compassion, gratitude.

Within Hope is strength, creative energy and a promise for an abundant life.

Some people aim for freedom from the past but this is only one half of the equation. The other half is joyful expectation for a beautiful, fulfilling and abundant future. I will use an analogy in utilizing these three concepts—Pray Big, Love Big and Hope Big. Sometimes in farming or driving accidents, the mishap occurs because of operator error. This operator error happens because the equipment is being used incorrectly. Many of us are experiencing operator error when we pray, love and hope.

"The real voyage of discovery consists not in seeking new landscapes, but in having new eyes."
Marcel Proust

We have within us the conditions necessary for inner happiness. We just have to find it, nurture it and live it. I realize the possibility that there may be other paths, parallel paths, which could lead to salvation. The one basic point in this theory is that the practitioner must follow his chosen path with truth. There are too many hypocrites in the churches, synagogues, temples, center, mosques, houses, and other places of worship. We must all return to the basics and this can be done by these three simple practices: Pray Big, Love Big and Hope Big!

<u>PRAY BIG</u>: Praying is so important because it's believing in something greater than ourselves. Effective prayer is about communication between us and our God. In prayer the medium is love, mindfulness and right thinking. All things good should go into prayer. I promote being mindful in order to move to the right place for effective prayer. In prayer our body and mind are directed to a single point, the present moment with God. So to pray big, one must dwell peacefully with honest intent in the present moment. Concentration should be on the good, the pure, the uplifting, the light!! Many people pray for the wrong things using negative energy. But prayer is about positive energy directed to the great force of good in the universe -- God. When one prays wrong or about wrong things, that energy is not positive; it becomes negative. We pray wrong when we seek things outside of God's will.

I mentioned earlier how EGO stands for edging God out. When we put our ego out front, we are in fact saying that God does not exist and that is all about us. Prayer is about faith and belief.

Prayer as a spiritual practice works. Prayer is about communicating with God. We reveal our innermost selves to ourselves through prayer. Many people are used to deceiving themselves. People have been so conditioned in life that they believe the illusions and are not able to live up to their inner potential because they fall for the illusions and delusions of life. The illusions are reinforced by the media and our environment. We fall for the delusions and illusions that surround us.

Albert Einstein stated, *"A human being is part of the whole called by us 'universe,' a part limited in time and space. He experienced himself, his thoughts and feelings, as something separated from the rest -- a kind of optical delusion of his consciousness. The delusion is a kind of prison for us, restricting us to our personal desires and to affection for persons nearest to us. Our task must be to free ourselves from this prison by widening our circle of compassion to embrace all living creatures and the whole of nature in its beauty."*

Prayer connects us with God and also to our fellow humans. In our daily lives our minds tend to think about the past or worry about the future. When we pray we force our mind and consciousness to stay in the present. The present is where we struggle to maintain connection. The Buddha taught, *"The past is already gone. The future has not yet come. Life can only be touched in the present moment."* When we can stay in the present moment, through prayer and meditation, we can be nourished and healed. Being right-minded by learning how to pray emits positive loving energy into the universe which turns back to the same person in blessings.

LOVE BIG: Love big, without limits! The main principle of being a Christian is love. Paul explains in Galatians 5:14, "The entire law is summed up in a single command, love your neighbor as yourself." Jesus, the Buddha and other holy men of old explained how love is the key to living life to the fullest.

Love is that self-less, deep and constant love which finds its greatest expression in the love of God and in the love that Jesus manifested on the cross. 1 Corinthians 13 provides a great explanation of love. It is described as patient, kind, and unselfish. It is not envious, boastful, proud or rude, not is it easily angered. Love rejoices in the truth. This love keeps no record of wrongs and does not delight in evil. These are also the characteristics of Jesus and should be our operating directive for how we operate in life.

The Buddha said the following: *"Hate is not conquered by hate. Hate is conquered by love. This is a law eternal."*

Saint Teresa of Areila stated that, *"Love draws forth love."*

The Sufi mystic Rumi's recurring theme was about the divine nature of love. Rumi explained that love is born from oneness with the divine and therefore is ultimately indefinable and beyond intellectual expression. Rumi believed that love has a cleansing effect on the soul. Love purges the mind of deep-seated illusions by helping it see that the oneness is the fundamental ground for all existence. Rumi suggests that this is a radically life-altering event. While no religion may possess truth in its entirety, each contains important pointers, reminders of where the truth may be found. But ultimately, we have to discover the truth ourselves. Truth is found in the depths of our own hearts. In order to understand what love is, we have to burn all the pollutants out of us. This is only done by becoming aware of all the conditioning we have endured. Awareness of one's own conditioned state is the beginning of wisdom.

Joy springs from love. If there is love then there will be joy, happiness and forgiveness. If you truly love your neighbor then you will forgive him/her because they are just as flawed as we all are. If we love, we have compassion for those who are less enlightened than we are. If we love, we would not judge others because love is about acceptance while judging is about not accepting others as they are. Judging is about pride and ego because we feel superior when we judge others. Love is the fulfillment of the law. Within a deep and pure agape love are forgiveness, compassion and gratitude.

St. Augustine explained it so simply, *"As love grown in you, beauty grows too. For love is the beauty of the soul."* Love is the highest energy we can pull out of ourselves. When we love, we are emanating truth, goodness, and pure intent.

My journey of growth and transformation would not have been possible if I did not connect to my spiritual core which was based in love. Love is powerful and has the creative force within it to cause miracles. Do not focus on loving that car or house. Focus on loving yourself, loving others, loving your day and loving your life.

1 John 4:7-8 states, "Beloved, let us love one another, for love is of God, and everyone who loves is born of God and knows God. He who does not love does not know God, for God is love." God is love -- wow! I read that verse and my heart soars because I am connecting with God when I love. I try to focus each day on emanating love, a deep and profound love without judgment.

Further in John 1:17-19 we learn the following: "Love has been perfected among us in this: that we may have boldness in the Day of Judgment, because as He is, so are we in this world. (Author's comment: There are so many powerful forces inside of us, it's a shame that most of us do not even realize it). There is no fear in love, but perfect love casts out fear, because fear involves torment. But he who fears has not been made perfect in love. We love Him because He first loved us."

God sees the potential in us because we are of God (1 John 4:4) and if God is love then we are love also. God wants us to not be conformed to this world but to be renewed by the transforming of our minds so that we may provide what is that good and acceptable and perfect will of God (Romans 12:2).

It does not matter what you have done or who you are because you are of God. You can ignite that fire within but you have to have love, you have to be love. When our heart is full of love, then we are creating more love, peace, and joy in the world. Love sent out is returned to us.

HOPE BIG: Strength for today and bright hope for tomorrow is one of my life mottos. We live in the present but we must plan for success. We plan for success by being prayerful and loving as mentioned above. Hope is so important in life. Too many people walk around in defeat expecting every bad things to come into their lives. Hope is about joyful expectation, expecting the best from others and from ourselves. It is the expectation of miracles coming into our lives. When we expect miracles we are practicing hope. Hope never disappoints, according to the Bible (Romans 5:5).

If prayer is about loving God and the universe, love is about loving ourselves and others, then hope is about loving our future. Hope is about having faith in a loving God who has our best interest at heart. God loves us and wants us to know Him.

Paul wrote about hope in the New Testament in Romans 8:19-25 states, "For the anxious longing of the creation waits eagerly for the revealing of the sons of God. For the creation was subjected to futility, not willingly but because of Him who subjected it in hope, that the creation itself also will be set free from its slavery to corruption into the freedom of the glory of the children of God. For we know that the whole creation groans and suffers the pains of childbirth together until now. And not only this, but also we ourselves, having the first fruit of the Spirit, even we ourselves groan within ourselves, waiting eagerly for our adoption as sons, the redemption of our body. For in hope we have been saved, but hope that is seen not hope; for who hopes for what he has already seen? But if we hope for what we do not see, with perseverance we wait eagerly for it."

In 2 Corinthians 4:18 Paul tells us that, "While we look not at the things which are not seen; for the things which are not seen are temporary, but the things which are not seen are eternal."

In Philippians 3:13-14 we obtain amazing wisdom from Paul regarding how to live our hope, "Brethren, I do not regard myself as having laid hold of it yet; but one thing I do: forgetting what lies behind and reaching forward to what lies ahead, I press on toward the goal for the prize of the upward call of God in Christ Jesus." Hope is not about dwelling on the past but understanding that we are forgiven through Jesus' sacrifice on the cross; thus me must move on to a life of faith and obedience.

"And we desire that each one of you show the same diligence so as to realize the full assurance of hope until the end, so that you will not be sluggish, but imitator of those who through faith and patience inherit the promises (Hebrews 6:11-12)." Thus in hope, we must be patient and have faith.

In Revelation 22:21 (the last sentence in the Bible), it reads, "The grace of the Lord Jesus be with all, amen." Revelation is a book about hope. It shows that no matter what happens on earth, God is in control and evil will not last forever. As believers we do not have to worry because we have hope in future glory. God has promised a new heaven and a new earth, so have hope!

James Allen said over 100 years ago, *"Our life is what our thoughts make it. A man will find that as he alters his thoughts toward things and other people; things and other people will alter towards him."*

"Our real wealth is in the intangible power of thought." Napoleon Hill

The Word of God is food for the soul so this chapter is called Fruits of the Spirit, and I offer you more fruit. In the three principles I mentioned earlier: Pray Big, Love Big, and Hope Big. The Holy Scripture details how these principles have power in them; "There are three things that endure –faith, hope and love (1 Corinthians 13:13)." We must be bold in our faith. God says in the Bible that we should come boldly to the throne of Grace. Being bold can add power to your life.

We have all had times in our lives when we were on fire for something; career, loved ones, a TV show, a musical group, etc., but it is only through having a bold, spirit-filled life that we can truly feel fulfilled. So many of us are too tired to go to church or read His word, but if there is anything we should seek out with enthusiasm, it is God. Be bold in your spiritual life.

So from the three principles: Pray Big, Love Big and Hope Big, add Boldness

Pray Boldly, Love Boldly, and Hope Boldly.

Pray BIG and PRAY BOLDLY on these scriptures:

"Call upon me in the day of trouble, I will deliver you, and you will honor Me (Psalm 50:15)."

"The Lord is near to all who call on Him, to all who call on Him in truth. He fulfills the desires of those who fear Him: He hares their cry and saves them (Psalm 145: 18-19)."

"It shall come to pass that before they call, I will answer, and while they are still speaking I will hear (Isaiah 65:24)."

"In these days when you pray I will listen. If you look for me in earnest you will find me when you seek me (Jeremiah 29: 12-13)."

"Whatever you ask in prayer, you will receive, if you have faith (Matthew 21:22)."

"When you pray, go to your room, close the door and pray to your father who is unseen. Then your Father, who sees what is done in secret, will reward you (Matthew 6:6)."

"The earnest prayer of a righteous person has great power and wonderful results (James 5:16)."

"While Jesus was here on earth, He offered prayers and pleadings, with a loud cry and tears, to the one who could deliver him out of death. And God heard His prayers because of His reverence for God (Hebrews 5:7)."

Meditation and prayer go hand-in-hand. The Buddhist often uses the following meditation exercise to begin their meditative practice. Breathe in and out of the stomach: when you inhale say the word 'calm' to yourself. With each exhale, say the word 'smile' to yourself. Meditation is a great way to prepare you for prayer. Prayer directs our consciousness to God. Through prayer we request assistance from the Divine. Prayer helps us to be humble. Prayer in and of itself brings inner healing and with faith outer healing can occur. Prayer brings guidance and releases tension. Pray BIG and BOLDLY!

LOVE BIG AND LOVE BOLDLY on these scriptures:

"I, the Lord your God, am a jealous God who will not share your affection with any other god! I do not leave unpunished the sins of those who hate me. But I lavish my love on those who love me and obey my commands, even for a thousand generations (Exodus 20 5:6)."

"I love those who love me; those who look for me find me (Proverbs 8:17)."

"A new command I give you: Love one another. As I have loved you so you must know that you are my disciples, if you love one another (John 13:34)."

"Eye has not seen, nor ear heard, nor have entered into the heart of man the things which God has prepared for those who love Him (1 Corinthians 2:9)."

The purest example of perfect love is the love of Jesus. On the cross, despite His agony of body, mind and soul, His thoughts were all for others. Even those who sought to torture, defile and humiliate Him came under His protection with these words, "Father, forgive them for they know not what they do (Luke 23:24)." Are we all trying to carry on this same type of love in our daily life?

"The love of God has been poured out into our hearts by the Holy Spirit who was given to us (Romans 5:5)"

"Everyone who believes that Jesus is the Christ is a child of God. And everyone who loves the Father loves His children, too. We know we love God's children if we love God and obey His commandments (1 John 5:1-2)."

HOPE BIG and HOPE BOLDLY on these Scriptures:

"Our hope is in the living God, who is the Savior of all people, and particularly of those who believe (1 Timothy 4:10)."

"Let us hold fast the confession of our hope without wavering, for He who promised is faithful (Hebrew 10:23)."

"He delivered us from such a deadly peril, and he will deliver us. On Him we have set our hope that He will deliver us again (2 Corinthians 1:10)."

"So be strong and take courage, all you who put your hope in the Lord (Psalm 31:24)."

"For you, O Lord, are my trust, O lord, from my youth (Psalm 71:5)."

"I pray also that the eyes of your heart may be enlightened in order that you may know the hope to which He has called you, the riches of His glorious inheritance in the saints, and His incomparably great power for us who believe. That power is like the working of His mighty strength (Ephesians 1:18-19)."

"For everything that was written in the past was written to teach us, so that through endurance and encouragement of the Scriptures we might have hope (Romans 15:4)."

"May the God of hope fill you with all joy and peace in believing, hat you may abound in hope by the power of the Holy Spirit (Romans 15:4)."

"The Lord is good to those whose hope is in Him, to the one who seeks Him (Lamentations 3:25)."

"Praise God, the Father of our Lord Jesus Christ. God is so good, and by raising Jesus from death, He has given us new life and a hope that lives on (1 Peter 1:3)."

We were all created by God for some great purpose. To achieve that high calling, we need to tame our ego and control our racing thoughts in order to stay on a path which is pleasing to God. We all need to be as bold as a lion for God like Peter. We need believe that God gave us the power for greatness. There are so many of us are living less than our Godly birthright. God intended that all gain in the glory of this life and the next life.

The Yoga sutras of Patanjali states: "*When you are inspired by some great purpose, some extraordinary project, all your thoughts break their bounds. Your mind transcends limitations, your consciousness expands in every direction, and you find yourself in a new, great and wonderful world.*"

God has given each of us all we ever need. We have it all already. Deep within every human is the spark to live a life of greatness but through the conditioning process I described earlier, we lose that fire. We grow to doubt ourselves. We learn to think defeating thoughts of ourselves. We forget whose we are---children of the Most High God who breathed His breath into us. That spark has been within us since our birth. The potential is inside of each of us. We can all regain that initial spark and turn it into a roaring fire by changing our thoughts and Praying Big and Bold; Loving Big and Bold; and Hoping Big and Bold!

It takes a conscious decision and effort to live a life of greatness with passion and enthusiasm. We can all be inspired. Living In-Spir-ed (In Spirit-ed) means that we harness the spirit inside of us.

We have the power and it is up to us if we want to choose life or death. God's greatest gift to us is free will. For some, however, this is their greatest curse.

"Most people search high and wide for the keys to success. If they only knew the key to their dreams lies within." George Washington Carver

I love this quote because it came from a man who understood this verse. Carver, a professor at Alabama's Tuskegee Institute, was able to offer a solution for the post-civil war farmers when the farm land in his area needed a solution for a depleted land where cotton had sucked all the nutrients out of the land. Carver proposed that the farmers change crops to restore nitrogen and fertility to the land. The farmers refused. The boll weevil came in and destroyed all the cotton crops so that farmer then had to do something different. Carver told the farmers to burn off the infested crops and plant peanuts. The people did not know what to do with them. Working day and night, Carver was able to turn a potential loss into a huge profit. In less than five years, peanut production turned that Alabama county into one of the wealthiest parts of the state. Carver was able to extract more than three hundred products from the peanuts.

Within all of us, is greatness!

Answers are always available to those who earnestly ask for them. All humans are as beautiful and as loved as they believe themselves to be (I repeat this so it will be internalized). It is about that power within. Anything is possible with earnest desire. We must build a mindset which no longer holds us back from what we desire. Who we can be is determined by our own awareness of ourselves. The only approval and acceptance that anyone ever needs is their own. Stop being a slave to what other people think of you. I have now learned that there are no mistakes in life, only learning experiences. I have the power and decide who I want to be in every moment. We were all created from an infinite source of love. We all have an unlimited potential to love. If we can understand that once we become aware then we can become more in balance with the universe. Becoming more aware of the unlimited power we all have inside of us to create can have a transformative effect on our lives. The Bible says, "Seek and you shall find." We must search and then accept the answers we learn in order to change.

Many of us are so afraid to look inside of ourselves because fear, guilt, shame, anger, regret and pride. Create a new internal directive for yourself. In order to transcend our conditioning, we have to question what has kept each of us from reaching our potential in the past. It was only through looking inside and making some changes did I eventually become free. Where there is faith, there is no fear. Prayer is faith in action and without action; the dream will remain just a dream.

Our greatest work should be done inside our thoughts. Pray, love and hope big! Aspire to achieve your dreams. There is great music inside of you waiting to come out. We can only dream lofty dreams when we pray, love and hope big and boldly!

Chapter 23

Summary of 20 Steps to Empowerment and Love

1 Timothy 6:12 says, Fight the good fight of faith..." I realized that I, along with many others, were fighting the wrong battles in our minds and in the world. At a lowest point in my life, I lost my job and became depressed, but I heard a voice I believe to be God's. The voice spoke to me and let me know that it was not the end but just the beginning, and I had more to accomplish before I left this world. From that state of mind, I started attending church several times a week, read the bible and books by great spiritual teachers like Joyce Meyers and Joel Osteen. I realized that the only way to find inner joy was to create a solid, spiritual foundation and serve God by helping others. Through this process, I found meaning and purpose in life. My 20 steps to love and Empowerment is a life plan centered on helping people navigate back to God, just as I had found my way back. Love is about opening our hearts, leaving our egos and past dysfunctions behind us. My plan centers on becoming a warrior of light and love.

"I shall light a candle of understanding in thine heart which shall not be put out." Apocrypha

In order to find inner peace, I had to develop internal healthy principles. God has given us all we need. I realized that I had all I needed already but I just had to get rid of the old programming. We used to think that the world was flat but through science and experimentation, we now know that its round. There was a time in the 15th and 16th centuries that some people when even presented with evidence that the world was round, still believed that it was still flat. Today, there are still people walking around today thinking the world is flat in certain parts of their lives. Those first explorers dared to think differently, and I dare you to set aside your preconceived beliefs in order to think differently. Most people are still bound by past hurts, traumas and conditioning. I realized that I was bound by my demons of my own making and I had to make a paradigm shift in my head. To make this shift, I had to replace my old habits with new healthier habits. Thus, my 20 steps were born. I devised a plan centered on God's wisdom. A new positive path helped me to reprogram myself; such as stated in Galatians 5:22-23, "But the fruits of the Spirit is love, joy, peace, longsuffering, kindness, goodness, faithfulness, gentleness, self-control..." My plan is about light because, "We grope...feeling our way like men without eyes (Isaiah 59:10)."

I prayed to God and was led to write about how my steps helped me, to possibly help others. I decided that anything I wrote would be to glorify God and to help lead others to God. I started seeing how I could help others view life through a God-Consciousness paradigm, ignite that inner fire while finding direction, meaning and purpose in their lives. I have now learned to accept all situations with a smile on my face. Through our challenges, we must learn to never lose hope because God is always in the background routing for us. The Apostle Paul stated from a Roman prison in Philippians 4:11, "I have learned to be content in whatever state I find myself." I have learned how to joyfully accept the challenges of life.

Too few people are "all in" but instead are "part-time" spiritual seekers. James 1:1-8 tells us that we should count it all joy when we fall into various trials because they help us grow. Compassion and acceptance leads to balance. Balance allows us to notice the small miracles of daily life. Every day I notice the birds singing and I imagine God speaking through those birds saying, "Stay strong", "Have faith!", "Help Others!", and "Continue to look for Our Father in every experience." I would normally see the birds as distractions but now I see myself connected to them and the trees because we were both created by God. I was able to eject the emotional rubbish of the past by studying how both the mighty oak and the lovely dogwood trees on my run in the morning in the park could endure through harsh weathers and thrive; if they could, so could I.

Staying teachable was a valuable point in this work. I believe God is constantly seeking to teach us. "All of us have sinned and come short of the glory of God... (Romans 3:23). I realized that it was okay to fail as long as I learned the lesson that God was trying to teach me from my failure. We can all accomplish great things for God, but it requires aforethought, focus and planning. God wants us to soar! I never knew what was important in life, having faith in God is the most important point of living on this rock.

Hebrew 11:6 tells us what pleases God, "But without faith it is impossible to please Him: for He that cometh to God must believe that He is, and that He is a rewarder of them that diligently seek Him." My 20 steps are founded in pleasing God. We should all attempt to make an impact for God. I realized that not only did I fight the wrong battles in my mind, I focused on the wrong things. God will do whatever He has to do to save us. It is not God's intention that any of us should be lost and go to hell. God loves each of us with unconditional love! I never fully understood this before. If God could love me and you then I could love myself and you too.

My 20 steps focused on cognitive restructuring our thoughts by identifying our previous thinking errors and developing a plan to reframe our thinking. All of my steps feed into one another and are based on principles from the Christian, Jewish, Hindu, Buddhist, and Islamic traditions. When God spoke to me, I believe His goal was to transform me to help others.

Once I started listening to God's voice, the quality of my life got better. Sometimes, God has to make a way for us to be still, so we can learn. God has something special for each of us to do in life but we must search ourselves in order to change. The choice is ours and we have the power inside of us. God is in us, but most of us have lost our way. Some say that Albert Einstein's whole goal was to find God. He said he wanted to know God's thoughts. At the end of his life, he stated that he didn't find God. We are born out of an environment of an unholy world which rewards the bad and in many ways ridicules the good.

"Success is living a life that makes a difference. The question to ask is whether or not the world is a better place because of your efforts." Anonymous

Through the process of my spiritual quest, I have learned and grown. We must all be seekers in order to find something. The quote above touched me because I believe it tells me how I want to live my life with a God-consciousness so I can spread more balance in the world.

Another anonymous quote states that, "*You are exactly where God wants you to be.*" Thinking about this quote allows me to live in the present moment and thrive regardless of my circumstances. God is in charge and He has a purpose for us. I started looking for the lesson in every experience and viewed each experience as another step closer to where God was leading me to. Too many people have a psychiatric or emotional void inside of them which they constantly try to fill with things. When they can't get those things, they feel incomplete. They try to fill that void with money, alcohol, drugs, collection of things, sex, approval of others, work and other external things but that void can only be filled by nurturing and maturing our spirituality.

Through my steps, I started to become content because I was following my destiny. I was now aiming better, aiming for heaven. I have accepted my path without complaining. Life teaches everyone, however long it may take. God's words tell us, "We are special." Once I noticed that the Hand of God was on my life, I could flourish.

Lift your head up and realize whose you are--God loves you and me the same. 1 Peter 2:9 states that we are a chosen generation...His own special people." My new spiritual goal is became "to be the man, God intended me to be." Also, understand that we are all successful because we always hit the target we aim for in life. Most of us don't aim high enough and some aim for failure or a corrupt, broken life. Once we start to habitually aim for higher virtues and goals, then our lives will get better.

When our aim is off then our lives are off. I found that the 20 steps anchored my life to a path of light and love. Much of the wisdom in the Bible is echoed in other spiritual traditions. In Buddhism, covetness leads to suffering just as Jesus tells us in Luke 12:15.

In Psalms 107:2 it says, "Let the redeemed of the Lord say so, whom He hath redeemed from the hand of the enemy." We learn in Ephesians 6:15-17, "See then that you walk circumspectly, not as fools but as wise, redeeming the time, because the days are evil. Therefore do not be unwise, but understand what is the will of the Lord is." We each have gifts from God inside of us (Romans 12:6). The only way to use those gifts to the fullest is live for God in the present moment. The past is gone; we can redeem that time by serving God and making every second count!

Make an impact for God!

John 10:10 states, "the thief comes to steal, kill and destroy but Jesus came so that we may have life and have it more abundantly." We have a choice before us: life or the illusion. We should not choose a life of mediocrity but a life of abundance and amazement. Deuteronomy 30:19

states, "...I have set before you life and death, blessing and cursing therefore choose life, that both you and your descendants may live."

God wants us to live, and have an abundant life!

Dare to think differently: Some of us have such strong negative thoughts in our head that it limits us, even cripples us, from living up to our potential. The only difference between us and Bill Gates or the late Steve Jobs is that they lived in a world of infinite possibilities. Winning athletes say, "I can," while those who are not winners say, "I can't or it's too hard or I'm too busy."

There are four stories which resonate deeply with me from the Bible: Moses, Joseph, Job and Paul.

--Moses was drawn out of the Nile. He went from living as a prince of Egypt for the first 40 years of his life, to becoming a murderer. Escaping out of Egypt and making his way to live in the Sinai for the next 40 years until he heeded the call of God. Moses listened to God and obeyed Him to become His messenger leading his nation to God.

--Joseph was his father's favorite son. His brothers sold him into slavery because they were jealous of him. He eventually ended up in Egypt where Potiphar's wife lied on him and stated that he had tried to have sex with her. He was imprisoned for many years. In prison, God stayed faithful to him and he was eventually freed. He rose to be the second most powerful man in Egypt and saved his family from starvation. Joseph told his brothers, who feared that he would get revenge on them, "Do not be afraid, for am I in the place of God? But as for you, you meant evil against me, but God meant it for good, in order to bring it about as it is this day, to save many people alive."

--Job was born in the land of Uz in Northern Arabia, next to Midian where Moses lived. Job lost it all but stayed faithful to God. The theme of Job's life resonated with me for many reasons. 1) There are things going on in heaven with God that believers know nothing about but which affect our lives; 2) We can't know the unknowable and it's useless to try to understand the mind of God; 3) God's people do suffer and bad things happen all the time to good people. Thus, no one can judge the spirituality of others based on their tragedies or successes; 4) God may seem far away but we are constantly in His mind. Perseverance in faith is important because God is good and we can confidently put our life in His hands; 5) The believer who is in the middle of a difficult circumstance should not abandon God but draw near to Him so that they may be comforted; and 6) Suffering may be intense but it will ultimately end for the righteous, and God will bless them abundantly. I find great guidance in Job's words in Job 1:21: "The Lord gave, and the Lord has taken away; Blessed be the name of the Lord." I echo his words, blessed be the name of the Lord!!

--Paul called himself the chief sinner (1 Timothy 1:15). Paul was a persecutor of the early Christians. Jesus appeared to him in a vision on the road to Damascus. Paul was privileged person, a Pharisee and a Roman citizen. He was also there when Stephen was stoned. He became the Apostle to the Gentiles, writing 13 books in the New Testament. Paul was a warrior of light and love. His writing on love in 1st Corinthians 13 shows what pure love is about. Paul, outside of our Lord Jesus, did more than anyone else to spread Christianity under the constant threat of torture, imprisonment and death. Paul endured a lot in life and there was no greater conversion in the New Testament than he.

Being focused: Our transformation must be the most important thing in our lives because as long as we are defective and dysfunctional, we will continue to spread darkness in the world. You can only be the person God intended you to be, by living in the light. Your purpose in life is connected to having balance which comes from being healthy in the physical, mental and spiritual areas. We need to be like the writer of Psalm 42:2 who say, "My soul thirsts for God, for the living God."

Parallel paths: Buddhists speak of oneness of body and mind, and about the three poisons that produce dissatisfaction or unhappiness. Poison 1: Ignorance of the truth, of how things really are without the dysfunction or illusion (similar to John 8:32 "And you shall know the truth and the truth shall make you free); Poison 2) Attachment to our possessions or accomplishments; and Poison 3) Aversion. The three poisons work together to create pain in our lives in this manner. Because we are ignorant of the truth, we think we can be made happy by having an attachment to a specific person, place, thing or feeling. We will always be disappointed by things and then aversion or anger, dislike or hatred with enter our lives. I learned some amazing truths in Buddhism while maintaining my faith and conviction in Christianity. My open mind allowed me to grow even more. Buddhism taught me that no one controls my destiny. I learned that it's all in my own hands and the potential for self-perfection is mine, right now. These concepts are in harmony with my Christian beliefs of seeking to imitate God.

The Theosophical Society (TS) also taught me a lot as well. Their message is centered on universal brotherhood, encouraging the study of comparative religion, philosophy and science, and to investigate unexplained laws of nature and the powers latent in man. One of the founders of the TS, Mme Helena Petrovna Blavatsky, stated "*that any human being who had reached a certain level of inner development and had enough courage and selflessness to tread the spiritual path could still find the door open to the gaining of a deeper insight into the mysteries of life and death, to the attainment of our spiritual purpose; that we could receive help from those who had gone far ahead of us.*" Further she explained, "*It was up to every one of us to unfold our inner potential to become the living embodiment of the divine spark within us. This is our birthright. At one stroke all the religions were shown as equal pathways to Truth, each being a chord in the universal symphony of human aspiration.*" Further, she provided more insight, "*There is a road, steep and thorny and beset with perils of every kind, but yet a road, and it leads to the heart of the Universe.*" We need to explore inner space, that place where the divine spark is hidden,

145

waiting for us to find it. The path to Truth needs courage and bravery because it's a supreme adventure.

More than 2000 years ago, Katha Upanishad stated, "*Awake, arise seek out the light. As narrow as the edge of a razor is the path that leads to the Eternal.*" This is similar to what Paul said in Ephesians in 5:14, "Awake you who are sleep, arise from the dead, and Christ will give you light." Wisdom from two different paths promoting consciousness and awakening. Earlier in Ephesians 5:8-10 we learn about the light, "For you were once darkness, but now you are in the light in the Lord. Walk as children of light (for the fruit of the Spirit is in all goodness, righteousness and truth), finding out what is acceptable to the Lord."

In today's tough economic times, too many people today are not only financially bankrupt but are also spiritually bankrupt and emotionally empty. These feelings lead to addictions to things because people are looking for an escape from reality or an illusion to take the pain away. Use of illegal drugs never helps anything. Actually addiction only blocks consciousness by promoting an escape to a path of untruth. Drugs takes a person into darkness instead of the light, death instead of life and unconsciousness instead of consciousness. Jesus said, "I am the light of the world. He who follows Me shall not walk in darkness, but have the light of life (John 8:12)."

My 20 steps helped me to awake. Once I awakened, life became more exciting. I have joy and a smile on my face every day because each day was like an Easter egg hunt because I started looking for God's hand and listening to His voice from the moment I wake up. I began to see God's hand routinely. My awareness was the beginning of real power entering my life. I learned that staying in the present moment and not the past or the future allowed me to find joy in the moment. Being mindful in all I did helped me. Mindfulness is the energy to be here and to witness deeply everything that happens in the present moment, aware of what is going on within and without. Both Buddhists and Christians know that nirvana or the Kingdom of God is within their hearts. There is great power in awakening!!

I wanted to list my favorite life verses from the Bible which helped me to stay on course. I have a section at the end of this work with a more comprehensive list of verses which will help you stay close to God.

Following the path: "Trust in the Lord with all your heart, and lean not on your own understanding; in all your ways acknowledge Him, and he shall direct your paths (Proverbs 3:5-6)."

What to do: "For I know the thoughts that I think toward you says the Lord, thoughts of peace and not of evil, to give you a future and a hope. Then you will call upon Me and go and pray to Me, and I will listen to you. And you will seek me and find Me, when you search for Me with all your heart. I will be found by you, says the Lord, and I will bring you back from your captivity, I will gather you from all nations from all places where I have driven you, says the

Lord, and I will bring you to the place from which I cause you to be carried away captive (Jeremiah 29:11-14)."

How to live: "...but one thing I do, forgetting those things which are behind and reaching forward to those things which are ahead, I press toward the goal for the prize of the upward of God in Christ Jesus (Phil 3:13-14)."

What we must do: "If you love Me, keep my commandments (John 14:15)."

How to be saved: "that if you confess with your mouth the Lord Jesus and believe in your heart that God has raised Him from the dead, you will be saved (Romans 10:9)."

We are tested: "...you were faithful over a few things, I will make you ruler over many things. Enter into the joy of your lord (Mathew 25:21)."

Be apart: "And do not be conformed to this world, but be transformed by the renewing of your mind, that you may prove what is good and acceptable and perfect will of God (Romans 12:2)."

Our mission: "You therefore must endure hardship as a good soldier of Jesus Christ (2 Timothy 2:3)."

Fulfill your ministry: "...Take heed to the ministry which you have received in the Lord, that you may fulfill it (Colossians 4:17)."

The enemy: "...the devil walks around like a roaring lion, seeking whom he may devour (1 Peter 5:8)."

How to combat the enemy: "Put on the whole armor of God... (Ephesians 6:10-11).

Life works as designed: "Do not be deceived, God is not to be mocked; for whatever a man sows, that he will also reap (Galatians 6:7-9)."

Power in us:

1) "I can do all things through Christ who strengthens me (Philippians 4:13)."

2) "You are of God, little children, and have overcome them, because He who is in you is greater than he who is in the world (1 John 4:4)."

3) "For our Gospel did not come to you in word only, but also in power, and in the Holy Spirit... (1 Thessalonians 1:5)."

Trials are important: "My Brethren, count it all joy when you fall into various trials, knowing that the testing of your faith produces patience (James 1:2-3)."

God is faithful: "So I will restore to you the years that the swarming locust has eaten (Joel 2:25)."

Love of God: "You shall love the Lord your God with all your heart, with all your soul and with all your mind. This is the first and the greatest law. And the 2nd is like the first, You shall love your neighbor as yourself (Mathew 22:37-39)."

God has our backs: "...Fear not, for I have redeemed you; I have called you by your name; You are Mine (Isaiah 43:1)." and "Since you were precious in My sight, you have been honored and I have loved you...Fear not, for I am with you...(Isaiah 43:4-5)"

Love fulfills the law: "Beloved, let us love one another, for love is of God; and everyone who loves is born of God and knows God. He who does not love does not know God, for God is love (1 John 4:7-8)."

Remember these last three thoughts on pray big, love big and hope big:

Pray Big: William McGill, an Episcopal priest explained it so elegantly, *"The value of persistent prayer is not that God will hear us... but that we will finally hear Him."*

Love Big: God so loved the world, that He gave his only begotten son (John 3:16)." The ultimate form of love is giving one's own son so the rest of us could have an opportunity for salvation.

Hope Big: *"Hope arouses, as nothing else can arouse, a passion for the possible."* William Sloan Coffin Jr., Senior Minister Riverside Church, NYC quoted in Christian Science monitor on 5 Jan 78.

Chapter 24

Mastery of Self

"Mastery of self should be our ultimate goal because it aligns our purpose with God's plans for our lives."

Once we gain some balance the goal is to Maintaining the insights and wisdom we have gained. This chapter provides clarity into how to continue to master ourselves on a daily basis. When we know better, we can do better. When we get better, it will get better. This chapter can help you lean into the light and be your best self.

Life is full of wonder and beautiful mysteries, but so many people either do not know this or have forgotten this fact. Each day, I look for the lesson God is trying to teach me with an open heart. Each day, seek the gifts that God is trying to bestow on you.

I previously discussed how Proverbs 23:7 was a life verse for me now. "For as a man thinketh in his heart, so is he." This verse allowed me to reconfigure my life along the spiritual lines which are pleasing to God. In the Gospel of Mark, Jesus repeats something similar when he says, "There is nothing that enters a man from outside which can defile him; but the things which come out of him, those are the things that defile a man (Mark 7:15)." This is expounded on in verses 20-23 when Jesus says, "What comes out of a man, that defiles a man. For within, out of the heart of men, proceed evil thoughts, adulteries, fornications, murders, thefts, covetousness, wickedness, deceit, lewdness, an evil eye, blasphemy, pride, foolishness. All the evil things come from within and defile a man." This is why it's so important to live that new life which is possible once we start to do things differently. Do something different today that is truly good for you.

I challenge the reader to do something radically different which you've previously have been reluctant to do: such as attending a Bible study, going to additional church service, reading the Bible today for an hour, go to a soup kitchen and volunteer, volunteer at your church today -- ask the minister what you can do even if its sweeping the floor, pray for that person you have a grudge against, praying that God blesses their life, call that friend or family member you have a resentment against, tell them you love them, be the light in the world that you want to see. This should be in addition to anything you are already doing, not in place of. The purpose of this exercise is to do something for someone else with honest intention, without the expectation of anything in return.

Our loving and merciful God "desires that everyone be saved and to come to the knowledge of truth" (1 Timothy 2:4). An anonymous author wrote the following short poem: *"A careless word may kindle strife, a cruel word may wreck a life; a timely word may lessen stress, a loving word may heal and bless."*

Proverbs 13:3 states, "He who guards his mouth preserves his life." We have the power to speak blessings over our life or death. It's your choice.

Choose an abundant life!

One way to move forward in a positive direction is to write a plan for your life for the next six months. For example, "Over the next six months, I plan to finish painting that room in my house, I plan to spend one hour a day working with my kids (Studies have shown that parents on average spent 20 minutes of quality time with their children each day. Our kids want our time, not our money or gifts. Time is the best gift any child can receive.) Or I plan to take two college courses towards my degree or obtain that cooking certificate, or write that book, or lose 20 pounds. Execution phase: Devote one hour a day to making that dream come true. The key to any good plan is specific and measureable results. I can measure losing weight or I can measure taking a college course.

The adversary (Satan) is always there waiting to bring us down. Satan uses people in our lives, sometimes Satan uses people who love us. Now these people are living a life of illusions just as we were before we decided to gain mastery of self. Once we gain mastery of ourselves and are able to escape the illusions, we can then help others come to the truth. It's like on a plane when the flight attendant tells us to put our oxygen mask on first before helping our children or others with their mask. We have to help ourselves first and then be gentle with others living in darkness so that we can bring others to the light. Thus do not be upset at those still living in the darkness, those who do not know how to master themselves.

Those living in darkness are still our best teachers. From those in the darkness, we are able to be reminded of what we do not want to be. Those who are not loving or those who get angry quickly or the prideful or the unforgiving need to be shown the way. We can be that light in the world. We need to understand what the devil is trying to do. The devil and his agents hate us. The devil wants to bring us down. The devil is targeting us each and every day. The devil is in a battle for our hearts and minds. The devil suits up each day in order to insert his programming into our heads. When we do not respond, the devil adjusts to make us uncomfortable or to take us away from our game plan. The devil hates humanity. The devil wants all of us to fall like he fell.

The devil has started a covert influence program against humanity. A covert influence campaign can only affect us if we remain unaware. The devil exists and hangs his hopes on people believing that he does not exist. I believe that some people do his bidding every day (some unwitting) just as the demons did years before. The devil wants to win our hearts and mind. The devil does not want you to master yourself. The devil wants you to be out of control in every way. The devil wants you to be petty, vengeful, unforgiving, ego-driven, envious, jealous, angry, hateful, and selfish as well as feeling any other negative feeling. The devil does not want you to look inside. The devil loves drift and procrastination. The devil inspires us to make excuses and to do anything else except read God's word. The devil wants you to be disagreeable and to lead a defeated life.

The devil's covert influence program would go something like this:

Name of operation: Battle for Humanity's Eternal Soul

Goal: To lead all humans to the pits of hell. To win the hearts and minds of the humans to do Satan's bidding.

Weapons available to the devil: Reality TV, tabloids, internet porn, depression, anything promoting idols (perhaps even a show U.S. or some other nation state with the name Idol in it), drugs/alcohol, hate, prejudice and narrow-mindedness.

Tools available to promote disbelief: Sin to include judging others, pride (a great tool), fear, selfishness, unforgiveness, anger, hatred, etc.

Budget: Unlimited resources

Difficulty in recruiting people to work against the humans: No difficulty

Opposition to goal: God gave the humans free will so we will not have to worry about Him. (Note, we will do another campaign to make people believe that there is no God. We will seek to keep people away from the churches or reading the bible. Look for opportunities to promote drugs and alcohol to aid in the permanent fall of man as this allows man to keep his hearts and minds away from God. Make people believe that they have no choice but to suffer.)

Potential Problems: Need to eliminate prayer, love, and hope in the world.

Devil's Motto: Life sucks or Blame God for all of your problems!

We cannot succumb to the devil's plan. With God, anything is possible because He gave us a choice. When I wrote this section, I started to get mad thinking about how the devil was trying to win my heart and mind. I think that we all need to get mad at what the devil is trying to do to us. The devil, the enemy, the adversary, the evil one, beelzebub and satan are all names for that force operating in the world pushing us to not live up to our potential. If depression is a tool used by the devil then Godly passion is a tool that God loves. God wants us to be passionate for Him and to love Him with all of our hearts, minds, soul, and strength. Do not give your hearts and minds to the devil. I know I gave mine to the devil for too many years but I took a step towards God.

If you take a step, then God will take a step towards you!

The thing about covert influence operations is that once those being influenced learn about the operation, it loses its effectiveness to influence. Thus, now you know that the devil is trying to influence you covertly without your knowledge, you can choose not to be a part of it anymore. Self-awareness will free you.

"Be still and know that I am God," from Psalm 46:10 lets us know that we need to slow down at times. The devil loves when we run around unfocused or focused on too many things. If we are unsteady in our mind then it's easy for the devil to win. We need to still our minds. We need to listen to what God is trying to say in our lives. God speaks to us through circumstances, people, biblical scriptures, sermons, and through spending quiet time with Him.

The devil does not want you or I to master ourselves. The devil sends distractions into our lives in order to take our focus off God. The devil loves when we blame God for crisis or tragedy. The devil does not like when we are excited about life and have hope.

Anthony Robbins in *Awaken the Giant Within* states, "*Too many of us leave ourselves at the mercy of outside events over which we may have no control, failing to take charge of our emotions -- over which we have all the control -- instead relying on short-term quick fixes (p.26)."* The devil loves short-term fixes. I like how Anthony Robbins talks about mastering oneself. He says that three decisions we all make every moment of our lives which control our destiny. *"1) Our decision about what we focus on; 2) Our decision about what things mean to us; and 3) Our decisions about what to do to create the results we desire (p.40)."* I found Anthony Robbins to be helpful in changing my life.

I developed a short cheat sheet of ABC's of Mastery of Self:

Assess your fearlessly to determine where you need work!

Believe in yourself because you are God's workmanship!

Choose life, happiness so you can have a better life!

Develop the qualities that make you better. Don't limit yourself!

Execute the necessary steps to achieve your goals!

Fix your stuff, fix your faults. If you don't deal with your stuff, then you force others to deal with it. Fight the right battles.

Good is the goal: You must think good thoughts, speak good words, and do good things all the time!

Hope Big and Boldly!

Invest in yourself-time, energy, and effort as well as others!

Jump up for life-get excited about life!

Kindness: Show kindness to yourself and others!

Love Big and Boldly! Laugh often!

Master yourself: body, mind, and spirit!

Never surrender to sadness or depression!

Open-minded to new ideas and beliefs. Open to change!

Pray Big and Boldly! Passion leads to power!

Question: Ask the right questions in order to change!

Recruit happiness by choosing your attitude each day and changing your habits!

Spot the issues of concern in your life and the conditioning of your past!

Take charge of your life!

Unleash the fire inside of you!

Victory is in Jesus Christ! A God consciousness leads to victory!

Winner: You are a winner!

X an unknown quantity in math -- X is the amount of love (unlimited) that can fit in your heart and that you can give to God and others.

Yearn for meaning and purpose in your life.

Zest for life! Live with a zest in your life!

I decided to make sure to provide a summary in the form of the ABC's so that people could master themselves so the devil's covert influence program would not be successful. If we look at the environment in which we live, the tricks of the devil become clearer. Use an infallible source, God's word in the Bible, to master yourself. The Bible contains details on the enemy and how to successful navigate the world we live in. The truth is readily available for those who seek it.

"On with the dance, let joy be unconfined," Mark Twain

'Know Better' Life Principle: **Don't let your circumstances define you, but let your circumstances motivate you.**

Albert Einstein said, *"We cannot solve our problems with the same thinking we used to create them.*

'Know Better' Life Principle: **Make Jesus Christ your life coach. Allow the teachings of Jesus rule over your life and you will see abundance flow into your life.**

Are you a follower of the crowd or God each day? God is looking for a chosen few to stand up and be an individual of faith.

I found two amazing poems about love I wanted to share:

--If the love Thou hast for me--

If the love Thou hast for me, Lord,

Is equal to my love for Thee,

Tell me why should life detain me?

And Thou, who dost me life afford?

--Soul, what requestest thou of me?

Dear Lord, only to see Thy face.

--And what dost thou most fear from thee?

What I most fear's to lose Thy grace.

Love all possessing is my quest,

Lord, take my heart and make it Thine,

Within Thy bosom build a nest

in a spot that meets Thy design.

My soul is God hidden so deep,

What else is left for it to crave,

But to love Thee more as Thy slave,

And in so loving, so to sleep,

Starting afresh Thy love to save.(Santa Teresa de Jesus 1515-1582)

--Pure Spirit--

Ferando de Herrera (1534-1597)

154

Pure Spirit! that within a form of clay

once veiled the brightness of Thy native sky;

In dreamless slumber sealed Thy burning eye,

Nor heavenward sought to wing thy flight away!

He that chastised thee did at length unclose

Thy prison doors, and give thee sweet release,

Unloose the moral coil, eternal peace

Received thee to its stillness and repose.

Look down once more from thy celestial dwelling,

Help me to rise and be immortal there---

An earthly vapor melting into air;--

For my whole soul with secret ardor swelling,

From earth's dark mansion struggles to be free,

And longs to soar away and be at rest with thee.

Self-improvement seems to be the purpose of having a spiritual foundation but too many people are content with the status quo. Once we move toward an all-powerful God, then God will move towards us.

Summary of "Know Better, Do Better, How to Lean into the Light" Process

The diagrams in the beginning of the book describe a process. I wanted to summarize the process of how to develop spiritually and strengthen the inner person so you can master yourself, and be your best self.

Spot or identify - the conditions in which we live; how the enemy works; how God's system operates; and who you are. The below verses of scripture in each section can provide some enlightenment.

--Romans 3:23 states, "For all have sinned and fall short of the glory of God."

--Romans: 6:23, "For the wages of sin is death, but the gift of God is eternal life in Christ Jesus our Lord."

--2 Timothy 4:5, "But be watchful in all things, endure affliction, do the work of an evangelist, fulfill your ministry."

--1 Peter 5:8, "Be sober, be vigilant; because your adversary the devil walks about like a roaring lion, seeking who he may devour."

--Galatians 6:7, "Do not be deceived, God i snot to be mocked; for whatever a man sow, that he will also reap."

--Romans 8:6, "For to be carnally minded is death, but to be spiritually minded is life and peace."

--Romans 8:28, "And we know that all things work together for good to those who love God, to those who are called according to His purpose."

Assess or analyze - yourself to include strengths and weaknesses, as well as your inner environment.

--1 Corinthians 11:28, "But let a man examine himself..."

--Galatians 6:4, "But let each one examine his own work..."

--2 Peter 3:11, "Therefore, since all these things will be dissolved, what manner of persons ought you to be in holy conduct and Godliness?"

--2 Timothy 3:16-17, "All Scripture is given by inspiration of God, and is profitable for doctrine, for reproof, for correction, for instruction in righteousness that the man of God may be complete, thoroughly equipped for every good work."

--1 Corinthians 16:14, "Let all that you do be done with love."

--Jesus said in John 8:32, "And you shall know the truth and the truth shall make you free."

Develop or restructure - your higher, Godly traits.

--Romans 12:2, "And do not be conformed to this world, but be transformed by the renewing of the mind, that you may prove what is good and acceptable and perfect will of God."

--2 Corinthians 10:5, "...Bringing every thought into captivity to the obedience of Christ."

--Jesus stated in Mathew 6:33, "But seek first the kingdom of God and His righteousness, and all things shall be added to you.

--Philippians 2:12, "...work out your own salvation with fear and trembling."

--Ephesians 6:10-11, "Finally, my brethren, be strong in the Lord and in the power of His might. Put on the whole armor of God, that you may be able to stand against the wiles of the devil."

--James 1:22, "But be doers of the word, and not hearers only, deceiving yourselves."

--Colossians 3:2, "Set your mind on things above, not on things on the earth."

Acquire - your desired results: inner peace, joy, abundance and a deep abiding relationship with God. Once Godly enlightenment is gained, we must maintain healthy spiritual habits to keep us on the path of light and love. Your best life will emerge when we master ourselves.

--Galatians 5:22-25, "But the fruit of the Spirit is love, joy, peace, longsuffering, kindness, goodness, faithfulness, gentleness, self-control. Against such there is no law... If we live in the Spirit, let us also walk in the Spirit."

--Colossians 3:14, "But above all these things put on love, which is the bond of perfection."

--1 Corinthians 13:13, "Now abide faith, hope, love, these three; but the greatest of these is love."

--2 John 1:8, "Look to yourselves, that we do not lose those things we worked for, but that we may receive a full reward."

--Ephesians 5:8, "For you were only in darkness, but now you are in the light in the Lord. Walk as children of light."

--1 Peter 2:9, "But you are a chosen generation, a royal priesthood, a holy nation, His own special people, that you may proclaim the praises of Him who called you out of darkness into His marvelous light."

I believe the process listed above, connected to the above anchoring Biblical verses, can assist anyone in getting closer to God will lead to an abundant life.

A SIMPLE PRAYER

Jesus, I know that I am Yours and You are mine forever.

Thank you for sending Your Spirit to me,

That I might have the power to live this new life with you.

Stir up your Spirit in me.

Release Your Spirit in me.

Baptize me with the fullness of Your Spirit;

That I may experience Your Presence and power in my life,

That I may find new meaning in Your Scriptures,

That I may find delight and comfort in Prayer,

That I may be able to love as You love and forgive as You forgive,

That I may discover and use the gifts you give me for the life of the church,

That I may experience the peace and the joy that You promised us,

Fill me with Your Spirit; Jesus, I wish to receive all that you have to give me.

Amen

Take this prayer, write it down and carry it with you at all times. Read it before you read the Bible daily and you will begin to see signs and wonders in your life. In this simple prayer are the spiritual keys to awakening greater power in your life! I pray that this prayer gives you the same comfort, serenity and inner peace that it has given me.

DISCUSSION GUIDE FOR BOOK CLUBS

This discussion guide provides questions and thoughts to stimulate a dialogue for book groups. There is also an attached ten part reader's guide to the Bible which I formulated to help lead others to Christ as it helped me gain a God consciousness.

I came to understand that honesty was the path to inner freedom which then led to self-awareness, all of which act as a protection against falling for the same illusions of the past. I realized how broken I was and that my brokenness would continue unless I did something radical about it. I decided to create a set of steps to restructure my thinking which focused on asking the right questions of myself. Self-awareness leads to transformation. I have to learn how to be truly honest with myself. It can be a challenge to move forward because sometimes it's painful to look inside but that is the only way one can grow into the people that God wishes us to be. I now embrace my weaknesses and it's a source of my strength. The strength being that it demands I continually strive forward in my life to stay on the right path; the path towards God. I hope by sharing my experiences, strength and hope with others that I am able to put a little light in the world where others can gain something positive from it.

1) The author discusses that he is led by a higher calling, to help others ignite that fire within. He states that he wants everyone to live up to their potential. Have you lived up to your potential?

2) Discuss of the 20 steps and how to integrate them into your life. Especially focus on love and forgiveness. What does loving with your whole heart means to you? Is there still unforgiveness in your heart? Do you understand which emotions and feelings are of God and of the evil one (the devil)?

7) Define love? What does love mean to you and what it is not? Do you actually live the way you define it? How can we love as God loves? How do you receive God's love on a daily basis? What does God's love look like to you? When the Bible says, "God is love", does your life say that you are a follower of God's path daily?

8) How kind are you on a daily basis? What does "making your religious practice mean to you?" Jesus tells us to be kind to those who mistreat us. Who is your circle has been unkind to you? What act of kindness can you show them today?

9) Discussion of the three major points in step 20: Pray Big, Hope Big and Love Big! Are you doing this on a daily basis?

10) Are there areas in your life that you could improve your prayer life, have a more hope and love in a bigger fashion?

Back Cover

Know Better, Do Better - 20 Steps to Empowerment and Love! by Philip Allan Turner is the author's second book. Maya Angelou stated, "I did then what I knew how to do. Now that I know better, I do better." This quote freed the author and allowed him to move forward after the most difficult time in his life. He believes this quote can provide inspiration to anyone who has made a mistake or fallen down. By knowing better, we can master ourselves so that we can our best self. After losing his job, his house and his life as he knew it, the author became severely depressed. He spent three years reading every self-help book he could and eventually found the Bible. This uplifting book uses spiritual wisdom to describe how we can become the people God intended us to be. The author made Jesus his life coach and was transformed. Using the Bible and other spiritual traditions, the author has devised 20 easy steps to love and empowerment. The first book in this series is called "Know Better, Do Better – How To Lean Into The Light and Be Your Best SELF!" and provides a complete strategy for living an abundant life. The author got so many positive responses from the first book; he created this summary version focused solely on the 20 steps.

The author puts forward five main premises throughout his books:

1) We are broken because of the conditioning we have gone through and the experiences we have lived;

2) There is another path, a more enlightened path;

3) Through effort and daily practice, we can break out of the programming of the past to rewire our minds to live a better life;

4) As salvation is not constant, neither is enlightenment. We must constantly strive to stay in the present moment and on the right Godly path; and

5) When we get better, it'll get better.

The author provides 'Know Better' Life Questions, 'Know Better' Life Principles along with 'Know Better' Empowerment Exercises to help the reader awaken to his purpose in life. This book can transform your life by challenging old beliefs.

###

Philip Allan Turner has held many jobs to include being a fitness instructor, a carpenter and a real estate agent, but now is focused on serving the Lord full-time. He writes spiritual non-

fiction, devotionals and historical fiction books. He is studying to be an ordained minister. He is from Philadelphia originally, but now calls Newark, N.J. home.